Lawrence Finch

Meditation Journey Ancient Wisdom Teachings to Mindful Living

By Lawrence Finch

Meditation Journey

© Copyright 2025 - All rights reserved.

The content contained within this book may not be reproduced, duplicated or transmitted without direct written permission from the author or the publisher.

Under no circumstances will any blame or legal responsibility be held against the publisher, or author, for any damages, reparation, or monetary loss due to the information contained within this book, either directly or indirectly.

Legal Notice:

This book is copyright-protected. It is only for personal use. You cannot amend, distribute, sell, use, quote or paraphrase any part, or the content within this book, without the consent of the author or publisher.

Disclaimer Notice:

Please note the information contained within this document is for educational and entertainment purposes only. All effort has been executed to present accurate, up to date, reliable, complete information. No warranties of any kind are declared or implied. Readers acknowledge that the author is not engaged in the rendering of legal, financial, medical or professional advice. The content within this book has been derived from various sources. Please consult a licensed professional before attempting any techniques outlined in this book.

By reading this document, the reader agrees that under no circumstances is the author responsible for any losses, direct or indirect, that are incurred as a result of the use of the information contained within this document, including, but not limited to, errors, omissions, or inaccuracies.

Lawrence Finch

Dedicated to the beautiful & lovely Caroline Yates

Meditation Journey

Lawrence Finch

© **Copyright 2025 - All rights reserved.** 2

Chapter 1: The Ancient Roots of Meditation: A Journey Through Time 1

    The Genesis of Eastern Meditation: India, A Cradle of Contemplation and Inner Inquiry 3

    Hinduism: From the Vedas to the Upanishads and the Nascent Stages of Yoga 4

    Buddhism: The Noble Eightfold Path and the Centrality of Meditation for Enlightenment 6

    Jainism: Meditation as a Path to Self-Control, Purification, and Ultimate Liberation 8

    The Subsequent Spread of Meditation Across Asia: A Rich Tapestry of Contemplative Traditions 9

    Key Philosophical and Spiritual Concepts Underpinning Early Meditation Practices 11

Chapter 2: The Buddhist Traditions of Meditation: A Tapestry of Mindfulness and Insight 15

    Vipassanā (Insight Meditation): The Art of Discerning Reality's True Nature 16

    Core Principles of Vipassanā: The Pillars of Insightful Awareness: 17

    Step-by-Step Instructions for a Basic Vipassanā Practice (Mindfulness of Breathing): 19

    Variations and Advanced Vipassanā Techniques: Deepening the Practice of Insight: 22

- Benefits and Potential Challenges of Vipassanā: Navigating the Path of Insight: 23
- Samatha-Bhāvanā (Concentration Meditation): Cultivating the Stillness of a Focused Mind: 24
- Core Principles of Samatha-Bhāvanā: The Foundations of Focused Tranquillity: 25
- Common Objects of Concentration in Samatha Practice: Anchors for the Focused Mind: 26
- Step-by-Step Instructions for a Basic Samatha Practice (Breath Concentration): 27
- Stages of Samadhi (Absorption): The Deepening of Mental Stillness: 28

Chapter 3: The Hindu Traditions of Meditation: A Multifaceted Path to Inner Realisation 31

- The Foundational Role of Yoga: Patanjali's Eight Limbs and the Path to Raja Yoga 32
- Patanjali's Eight Limbs of Yoga and Their Relation to Meditation: 32
- Step-by-Step Instructions for a Basic Raja Yoga Meditation (Focus on Breath): 34
- Bhakti Yoga: The Path of Devotion and Surrender Through Meditation 35
- Key Practices in Bhakti Yoga Meditation: 36
- Step-by-Step Instructions for a Basic Bhakti Yoga Meditation (Mantra Japa): 37

Jnana Yoga: The Path of Wisdom and Self-Inquiry Through Meditation 38

Key Practices in Jnana Yoga Meditation: 38

Step-by-Step Instructions for a Basic Jnana Yoga Meditation (Self-Inquiry - "Who am I?"): 39

Karma Yoga: The Path of Selfless Action Through Mindful Engagement 40

Key Principles of Karma Yoga Meditation: 40

Integrating Karma Yoga into Daily Life as Meditation: ... 40

The Interconnectedness of Hindu Meditation Traditions 41

Chapter 4: Beyond India: The Meditative Landscapes of Jainism and Other Eastern Traditions 43

Jainism: The Rigorous Path of Self-Discipline and Meditation for Liberation 44

Key Meditative Practices in Jainism: 44

Step-by-Step Instructions for a Basic Jain Meditation (Samayika - Focused Reflection): 46

Taoism: The Flow of the Tao and the Cultivation of Inner Harmony 47

Key Contemplative Practices in Taoism: 48

Step-by-Step Instructions for a Basic Taoist Contemplation (Breath and Lower Dantian): 49

Confucianism: Cultivating Virtue and Social Harmony Through Self-Discipline 50

Meditation Journey

Contemplative Aspects of Confucianism: 50

A Simple Confucian Practice of Self-Reflection: 51

Japanese Traditions: Zen and the Art of Mindful Presence 52

Key Meditative Practices in Zen Buddhism: 52

Step-by-Step Instructions for Basic Zazen (Seated Meditation): 53

Chapter 5: The Rise of Secular Mindfulness: Bridging Ancient Wisdom and Modern Science 57

Key Figures and Foundational Developments in Secular Mindfulness: 57

Core Principles and Techniques of Secular Mindfulness: 60

Diverse Applications of Secular Mindfulness in Modern Life: 62

The Scientific Basis of Secular Mindfulness: 64

Distinguishing Secular Mindfulness from Its Traditional Roots: 65

Potential Challenges and Considerations for the Future of Secular Mindfulness: 66

Chapter 6: Cultivating Mindfulness in Daily Life: Weaving Awareness into the Fabric of Existence 69

The Importance of Extending Mindfulness Beyond Formal Practice: 70

Strategies for Integrating Mindfulness into Daily Activities: 70

Cultivating Mindfulness in Challenging Situations: 73

Common Obstacles to Daily Mindfulness and How to Overcome Them: 74

The Long-Term Benefits of a Mindful Life: 75

Chapter 7: The Heart Practices: Cultivating Loving-Kindness and Compassion Through Meditation 77

Understanding Loving-Kindness (Mettā): The Foundation of Goodwill 78

Key Principles of Loving-Kindness: 78

Step-by-Step Instructions for Loving-Kindness Meditation: 79

Understanding Compassion (Karuṇā): The Wish to Alleviate Suffering 82

Key Principles of Compassion: 82

Step-by-Step Instructions for Compassion Meditation: 82

The Interconnectedness of Loving-Kindness and Compassion: 85

Benefits of Loving-Kindness and Compassion Meditation: 85

Challenges in Cultivating Loving-Kindness and Compassion: 86

Integrating Loving-Kindness and Compassion into Daily Life: 87

Chapter 8: Finding Stillness in Motion: The Practice of Movement-Based Meditation 89

The Innate Connection Between Movement and Awareness: 89

Key Principles of Movement-Based Meditation: 90

Exploring Different Forms of Movement-Based Meditation: 91

Step-by-Step Instructions for Walking Meditation: 92

Key Aspects of Mindful Yoga Practice: 93

Core Principles of Tai Chi and Qigong: 94

Key Aspects of Mindful Dance: 95

Benefits of Movement-Based Meditation: 96

Challenges and Considerations in Movement-Based Meditation: 97

Integrating Movement-Based Meditation into Your Life: 98

Chapter 9: The Guiding Voice and the Inner Eye: Exploring Guided Meditations and Visualisations 101

The Nature and Benefits of Guided Meditation: 101

Exploring Different Types of Guided Meditations: 103

The Power and Potential of Visualisation Meditation: . 104

Key Principles of Effective Visualisation: 105

Types and Techniques of Visualisation Meditation: 105

Integrating Guided Meditations and Visualisations into Your Practice: 107

Potential Challenges and How to Navigate Them: 108

Chapter 10: Meditation as a Tool for Transformation: Addressing Specific Challenges 111

Meditation for Anxiety: Cultivating Calm in the Face of Worry 111

Specific Practices for Anxiety: 112

Meditation for Depression: Finding Light in the Darkness 113

Specific Practices for Depression: 114

Meditation for Chronic Pain: Finding Peace Amidst Discomfort 115

Specific Practices for Chronic Pain: 116

Meditation for Sleep Disturbances: Cultivating a Calm Mind for Rest 116

Specific Practices for Sleep: 117

Meditation for Trauma: Gentle Presence and Reconnection 117

Specific Practices for Trauma (with professional guidance): 118

Important Considerations and Precautions: 119

Chapter 11: Deepening Your Meditation Practice: Cultivating Sustained Presence and Insight 121

Refining Your Core Technique: 121

Exploring Different Meditation Methods: 123

Cultivating Supportive Qualities: 124

Meditation Journey

- Navigating Deeper States and Experiences: 125
- Deepening Your Practice Off the Cushion: 126
- Seeking Guidance and Community: 127
- The Ongoing Journey: 127

Chapter 12: The Scientific Landscape of Meditation: Unveiling the Evidence 129

- The Rise of Scientific Inquiry into Meditation: 129
- Methodologies Employed in Meditation Research: 130
- Key Findings Across Various Domains: 131
  - Brain Structure and Function: 132
  - Stress Reduction and Mental Health: 133
  - Attention and Cognitive Function: 133
  - Pain Management: 134
  - Sleep: 134
  - Compassion and Prosocial Behaviour: 135
  - Ageing and Longevity: 135
- Mechanisms of Action: How Does Meditation Work? . 136
- Challenges and Future Directions in Meditation Research: 137

Lawrence Finch

Chapter 1: The Ancient Roots of Meditation: A Journey Through Time

Our yearning for self-understanding, grasping reality's essence, and attaining inner peace is a thread woven through the very fabric of human consciousness. Long before the advent of psychology or the groundbreaking discoveries of neuroscience, our ancestors across the globe instinctively engaged in practices that sought to quiet the incessant chatter of the mind, cultivate a heightened state of awareness, and establish a connection with something transcending the individual self. These primordial stirrings of contemplative practices represent the deep and ancient wellspring from which the diverse and multifaceted tradition we now recognise as meditation has sprung. To truly appreciate meditation's profound depth and enduring significance, we must embark on an extensive journey back through the corridors of time, meticulously tracing its origins through the enigmatic mists of prehistory and the flourishing of the earliest organised civilisations.

While pinpointing the precise moment and geographical location of the very first meditative act remains an impossibility, lost to the unrecorded epochs of human existence, the fields of archaeology and anthropology offer tantalising glimpses into early human behaviours that strongly suggest a nascent form of inner exploration. Consider the awe-inspiring cave paintings discovered in various parts of the world, masterpieces of prehistoric art depicting human figures in what appear to be trancelike states. Often surrounded by depictions of animals and otherworldly entities, these individuals may have been shamans or spiritual practitioners engaged in rituals to alter their consciousness for spiritual and practical purposes, seeking guidance, healing, or connection with the spirit world. The rhythmic chanting, the hypnotic beat of drums crafted from animal hides, and the repetitive, ritualistic movements frequently associated with shamanistic practices could be interpreted as rudimentary yet powerful forms of focused attention, the very bedrock upon which many later meditative techniques would be built. These early humans, living in an intimate and often precarious relationship with the natural world, likely found moments of profound stillness and keen observation to be beneficial and crucial for survival. Such moments would have fostered a primal awareness of their immediate surroundings, the subtle cues of the environment, and, perhaps intuitively, their own internal states of alertness and calm.

    As human societies gradually evolved from nomadic hunter-gatherer bands to more settled agricultural communities, and as the complexities of social structures began to emerge, their contemplative practices underwent refinement and formalisation. In the fertile crescents of Mesopotamia, cradling the dawn of civilization, and along the life-giving Nile Valley of ancient Egypt, while grand empires rose to prominence and inevitably crumbled into the sands of time, subtle yet persistent whispers of inner reflection can be discerned within surviving religious texts and artistic representations. Ancient Egyptian priests, custodians of esoteric knowledge and intricate rituals, undoubtedly engaged in prayers and ceremonies that likely involved focused attention, specific postures, and perhaps even altered states of consciousness, all aimed at fostering communion with their pantheon of deities and maintaining cosmic harmony. Similarly, the complex religious systems of Mesopotamia, with their emphasis on divination, the interpretation of omens, and the arduous task of understanding the often-inscrutable will of the gods, may have incorporated practices akin to contemplation – periods of focused mental engagement and seeking inner guidance. However, it is within the spiritual and philosophical traditions that blossomed in the East, particularly on the Indian subcontinent, that we find the most profound and direct lineages of meditation as we understand it today, with systematic frameworks and detailed instructions for cultivating inner awareness and transforming the very fabric of the mind.

The Genesis of Eastern Meditation: India, A Cradle of Contemplation and Inner Inquiry

The Indian subcontinent stands as a pivotal and fertile ground in meditation's long and intricate history. Here, within the ancient and deeply interconnected traditions of Hinduism, Buddhism, and Jainism, we encounter the earliest systematic frameworks, the most detailed instructions, and the most enduring legacies for the deliberate cultivation of inner awareness and the profound transformation of the human mind. The very seeds of meditative practice, sown in the rich and fertile soil of Indian spirituality, would eventually take root, blossom in diverse forms, and spread their influence across the vast expanse of Asia, and much later, across continents to the West, shaping countless lives and philosophical systems.

Hinduism: From the Vedas to the Upanishads and the Nascent Stages of Yoga

The deepest roots of Hindu meditation can be traced back to the most ancient and revered scriptures of India, the Vedas, which began to emerge around the period of the 15th to the 5th centuries BCE. While the early Vedas primarily focus on hymns of praise to the deities, elaborate ritualistic practices designed to maintain cosmic order, and complex cosmological narratives, they also contain subtle yet significant hints of introspective practices and a deep reverence for inner experience. The fundamental concept of *rita*, the inherent cosmic order and the principle of righteousness, and the emphasis on the importance of aligning the individual self with this universal order, strongly suggest an early awareness of the need for inner harmony, self-regulation, and a profound understanding of one's place within the larger cosmic scheme.

The Upanishads, a collection of profound philosophical texts that form the later strata of the Vedas (roughly 8th to 4th centuries BCE), mark a significant and transformative shift in emphasis towards more explicitly philosophical and deeply contemplative inquiry. These seminal texts delve into the very nature of the Self (*Atman*), the individual soul or essence, and its intricate and ultimately unified relationship with the ultimate, all-pervading reality known as *Brahman*. Practices such as *upasana*, which encompass various forms of meditation or focused contemplation on a chosen deity, a sacred symbol, or a profound philosophical concept, and the systematic exploration of inner states of consciousness, are explicitly discussed as crucial pathways to directly realising this fundamental unity between the individual and the universal. The Upanishads place a profound emphasis on the critical importance of self-knowledge, the direct experiential understanding of one's true nature, and the transcendence of the limited and often illusory ego, themes that would resonate deeply and find further elaboration in later meditative traditions across various schools of thought.

Within this intellectually fertile and spiritually charged Upanishadic context, the early seeds of what would eventually become the comprehensive Yoga system begin to sprout and take root. The very word "yoga" itself, derived from the ancient Sanskrit root "yuj," meaning "to yoke," "to join," or "to unite," signifies the fundamental aim of the practice: the conscious union of the individual self with the universal consciousness, the bridging of the perceived gap between the inner and the outer realms. While the classical Yoga Sutras of Patanjali, which emerged much later (around the 2nd century CE), provide a far more systematised and comprehensive philosophical and practical framework for the eight limbs of yoga, including asana (physical postures) and pranayama (breath control) as preparatory stages for deeper meditative practices, the Upanishads lay the essential groundwork by emphasising practices involving the conscious regulation of breath (*pranayama*) and the sustained focus of attention as indispensable means to quiet the restless mind and prepare it for the deeper states of contemplation (*dhyana*) that lead to profound insight. The Upanishads describe various early techniques for intentionally focusing the mind, such as sustained concentration on a single point of awareness, the rhythmic recitation of sacred syllables or mantras, and the deep contemplation of fundamental philosophical truths. These early yogic practices were not merely physical exercises, as they are often perceived in the modern West. They were deeply and intrinsically intertwined with profound philosophical inquiry and the ultimate pursuit of spiritual liberation (*moksha*) from the cycle of birth and death and the limitations of the ego.

Buddhism: The Noble Eightfold Path and the Centrality of Meditation for Enlightenment

Buddhism, a transformative spiritual tradition that emerged in India around the 6th century BCE with the awakening of Siddhartha Gautama (who became known as the Buddha, the "Enlightened One"), placed the practice of meditation at the very heart of its noble eightfold path to liberation from the pervasive suffering inherent in the human condition. The Buddha's own profound journey to enlightenment is said to have culminated in a deep and transformative meditative experience under the Bodhi tree, a pivotal event that shaped the course of his teachings and the future of a global spiritual tradition. Following his awakening, the Buddha taught extensively and systematically on the fundamental principles of mindfulness (*sati*) and concentrated attention (*samadhi*) as essential and indispensable tools for gaining a direct understanding of the true nature of suffering, its origins, its cessation, and the path leading to that cessation – ultimately, the attainment of liberation (*nirvana*).

Two primary and interconnected categories of Buddhist meditation practices emerged from the Buddha's teachings and the subsequent development of Buddhist philosophy: *Vipassanā* (insight meditation) and *Samatha-Bhāvanā* (concentration or tranquillity meditation). *Vipassanā* aims at developing profound insight into the fundamental characteristics of reality – its impermanent (*anicca*) nature, its inherent unsatisfactoriness or suffering (*dukkha*), and the absence of a permanent, independent self (*anatta*) – through the sustained and non-reactive mindful observation of thoughts, feelings, and sensations as they arise and inevitably pass away. *Samatha-Bhāvanā*, on the other hand, focuses on the deliberate cultivation of sustained and unwavering attention on a single object of focus, such as the breath, a mantra, or a visual image, with the primary aim of developing mental stability, clarity, and a profound sense of inner tranquillity. While distinct in their primary focus, these two core practices are often viewed within the Buddhist tradition as complementary and ultimately integral to the path of awakening. A calm and concentrated mind, cultivated through Samatha, provides the necessary stability for the penetrating insights of Vipassanā to arise.

The early Buddhist scriptures, such as the Pali Canon, which preserves the earliest recorded teachings of the Buddha, provide detailed and practical instructions on a wide range of meditative techniques. The *Satipaṭṭhāna Sutta* (Discourse on the Foundations of Mindfulness) is a particularly significant and foundational text, meticulously outlining the four key domains or foundations of mindfulness practice: mindfulness of the body (*kāyānupassanā*), mindfulness of feelings (*vedanānupassanā*), mindfulness of mind (*cittānupassanā*), and mindfulness of mental objects (*dhammānupassanā*). These comprehensive teachings emphasise the critical importance of cultivating a non-judgmental, present-moment awareness across all aspects of our experience, allowing us to observe reality as it truly is, without the distorting filters of our habitual reactions and preconceived notions.

Meditation Journey

As Buddhism spread rapidly throughout Asia, carried by dedicated monks, enthusiastic scholars, and intrepid merchants along the Silk Road and across vast geographical landscapes, its core meditative practices adapted and evolved as they encountered different cultures and interacted with existing indigenous traditions. In Southeast Asia, the Theravada school of Buddhism diligently preserved many of the early meditative techniques and teachings. In East Asia, Buddhism interacted profoundly with indigenous philosophies such as Taoism and Confucianism, giving rise to unique and influential forms of meditation within Chan (Zen) Buddhism, which emphasises direct experience, intuitive understanding, and practices like *zazen* (seated meditation) and *koan* contemplation (paradoxical riddles designed to break down conceptual thinking). In the high altitudes of Tibet, Tibetan Buddhism developed a rich and intricate tapestry of tantric practices, including elaborate visualisation meditations, the powerful recitation of mantras, and the transformative practice of deity yoga, all aimed at accelerating the process of transforming consciousness and realising one's inherent Buddha-nature.

Jainism: Meditation as a Path to Self-Control, Purification, and Ultimate Liberation

Jainism, another ancient and influential Indian religion that coexisted and interacted with early Buddhism, also places a significant and central emphasis on the practice of meditation as a crucial means to purify the soul (*jiva*) of karmic impurities and ultimately achieve liberation (*moksha*) from the cycle of birth and death. Jain philosophy centres on the profound concept of *karma* not merely as action but as a subtle, sticky substance that clings to the soul, obscuring its true and inherent nature – its infinite knowledge, bliss, and power. Meditation in Jainism is therefore viewed as an exceptionally powerful tool for diligently shedding the accumulated layers of karmic substance and realising the soul's intrinsic purity, boundless knowledge, and inherent bliss.

Jain meditative practices often involve rigorous self-discipline, a profound commitment to non-violence (*ahimsa*) in thought, word, and deed, and a deep cultivation of detachment from worldly possessions and even internal states. Core techniques include *Samayika* (a dedicated period of equanimity and deep self-reflection), various forms of *Dhyan* (encompassing different types of concentration and contemplation), and specific practices aimed at meticulously observing and understanding one's own thoughts and emotions without any form of attachment or judgment. Jain monks and nuns often engage in extensive periods of meditation, sometimes adopting challenging physical postures for prolonged durations, all in the service of cultivating unwavering mental fortitude, profound spiritual insight, and the ultimate purification of consciousness through diligent and sustained inner work. The central focus remains on achieving complete self-mastery and the radical purification of consciousness as the pathway to liberation.

The Subsequent Spread of Meditation Across Asia: A Rich Tapestry of Contemplative Traditions

As these core Indian traditions of Hinduism, Buddhism, and Jainism took firm root and flourished within their native soil, their diverse and powerful meditative practices embarked on transformative journeys across the vast expanse of Asia, carried by the dedicated footsteps of wandering monks, the insightful minds of traveling scholars, and the worldly endeavours of adventurous merchants. The ancient Silk Road, a vital artery connecting East and West, became not only a conduit for exchanging material goods but also a crucial pathway for transmitting profound spiritual ideas and transformative practices.

In China, as mentioned earlier, Buddhism encountered and interacted deeply with indigenous philosophical and spiritual systems like Taoism and Confucianism, leading to the emergence of unique and syncretic forms of meditation within Chan (Zen) Buddhism. Taoism possessed its own rich and ancient tradition of contemplative practices aimed at cultivating inner harmony, aligning oneself with the natural and effortless flow of the Tao, and ultimately achieving longevity and even spiritual immortality. These Taoist practices often involved sophisticated breathwork techniques, vivid visualisation, and the skilful cultivation of inner energy (*Qi*). While primarily focused on social ethics, ritual propriety, and the cultivation of virtue within a hierarchical social structure, Confucianism also emphasised the critical importance of self-cultivation and rigorous mental discipline, which can be seen as having significant meditative undertones.

Buddhism developed its unique and powerful Vajrayana or Tantric tradition in Tibet's high-altitude landscape. This tradition incorporates elaborate and transformative visualizations, the resonant recitation of potent mantras, and intricate ritual practices as powerful tools for accelerating the process of spiritual awakening. The profound concept of the *mandala* (sacred geometric diagrams representing the cosmos and the psyche) became a central focal point for complex and transformative visualisation meditations aimed at directly altering one's perception of reality and realising the interconnectedness of all phenomena.

Across Southeast Asia's diverse cultures, various schools of Buddhism, primarily the Theravada tradition, continued to emphasise the core practices of mindfulness and concentration, preserving many of the earliest meditative techniques. Developing specific and nuanced meditation techniques and establishing influential monastic centres were crucial in preserving and propagating these ancient contemplative traditions.

Key Philosophical and Spiritual Concepts Underpinning Early Meditation Practices

Underlying the diverse array of early meditation practices that emerged across these ancient traditions are several recurring and fundamental philosophical and spiritual concepts that provide a cohesive framework for their practice and articulate their ultimate goals:

- **The Nature of the Self:** Many traditions grappled with the fundamental question of the nature of the individual self, often seeking to transcend the limitations of the ego and realise a deeper, more universal, or even non-existent sense of identity.
- **The Problem of Suffering:** The profound recognition of suffering as an inherent and fundamental aspect of the human condition and the earnest quest for liberation from this pervasive

suffering served as a central driving force behind many meditative paths.
- **The Primacy of Awareness:** Deliberate cultivation of heightened awareness of one's inner and outer experiences, approached with a stance of nonjudgmental observation, was consistently seen as crucial for gaining profound insight and a deeper understanding of reality.
- **The Transformative Role of the Mind:** The mind was often viewed as the source of both suffering and the potential for liberation, and meditative practices were meticulously designed to train, discipline, and ultimately transform its often turbulent nature.
- **The Goal of Liberation or Enlightenment:** Many early meditative traditions aimed to achieve a profound state of liberation from the cycle of suffering and the limitations of the ego, often described as enlightenment, nirvana, or moksha.
- **The Interconnectedness of All Things:** Certain traditions emphasised the fundamental interconnectedness of all beings and all phenomena, and meditation was often seen as a direct pathway to realising this underlying unity.
-

In conclusion, the ancient roots of meditation are deep, complex, and intricately intertwined with humanity's earliest attempts to understand the mysteries of the self and our place within the vastness of the cosmos. From the subtle hints found in prehistoric rituals to the sophisticated and systematic frameworks developed within Hinduism, Buddhism, and Jainism, the enduring quest for inner peace, self-realisation, and liberation through contemplative practices has been a persistent and vital thread in the rich tapestry of human history. These early traditions laid the essential groundwork for the diverse forms of meditation practised across the globe today, offering timeless wisdom and profound insights into the nature of the human mind and the enduring path to inner transformation. As we move forward in this book, we will delve deeper into the specific practices that emerged from these ancient roots, exploring their unique characteristics, underlying principles, and enduring relevance in the complexities of the modern world.

Meditation Journey

Chapter 2: The Buddhist Traditions of Meditation: A Tapestry of Mindfulness and Insight

Emerging from the rich and multifaceted spiritual landscape of ancient India, the profound teachings of Siddhartha Gautama, the historical figure who became revered as the Buddha, irrevocably altered the course of contemplative practices worldwide. The Buddha's transformative experience of enlightenment, achieved through intense and dedicated meditative absorption, served as the cornerstone of his subsequent teachings. This pivotal event underscored the immense power inherent in the disciplined cultivation of a focused and acutely aware mind as the primary pathway to liberation from the pervasive cycle of suffering that he identified as the fundamental predicament of human existence. Over the ensuing centuries, as the Buddha's teachings spread across Asia's diverse cultures and geographical landscapes, a remarkably rich and varied array of meditation practices blossomed within the broader Buddhist tradition. Each distinct yet interconnected approach offered unique methodologies and philosophical underpinnings for cultivating insight, fostering profound tranquillity, and ultimately realising the ultimate goal of awakening. This chapter will explore some of the foundational and influential Buddhist meditation techniques, meticulously tracing their historical development, carefully examining their core principles, and providing more comprehensive and step-by-step instructions for engaging in these transformative practices.

Vipassanā (Insight Meditation): The Art of Discerning Reality's True Nature

Vipassanā, a Pali term often translated with nuanced meanings such as "insight," "clear seeing," or "penetrative understanding," stands as a central and foundational pillar of Buddhist meditation, holding a particularly prominent position within the Theravada tradition, which considers itself the oldest and most direct lineage preserving the Buddha's original teachings. The historical roots of Vipassanā practice can be traced directly and unequivocally back to the core teachings of the Buddha himself, most notably and comprehensively articulated within the seminal *Satipaṭṭhāna Sutta* (Discourse on the Foundations of Mindfulness). This profoundly influential text meticulously outlines the four fundamental foundations of mindfulness that serve as the very framework for Vipassanā practice: mindfulness of the body (*kāyānupassanā*), mindfulness of feelings or sensations (*vedanānupassanā*), mindfulness of the mind or states of consciousness (*cittānupassanā*), and mindfulness of mental objects or phenomena (*dhammānupassanā*). The overarching aim of consistent and dedicated Vipassanā practice is to cultivate a sustained, non-reactive, and unwavering present-moment awareness across these four crucial domains of human experience. Through this diligent and impartial observation, practitioners gradually develop a deep and experiential understanding of the three fundamental characteristics that the Buddha identified as inherent to all conditioned phenomena: impermanence (*anicca*), the inherent unsatisfactoriness or suffering (*dukkha*), and the absence of a permanent, independent self or essence (*anatta*). These insights are not merely intellectual understandings grasped through philosophical reasoning but rather profound and transformative experiential realisations that have the potential to fundamentally alter one's relationship with oneself and the entirety of reality, ultimately leading towards liberation from suffering.

Core Principles of Vipassanā: The Pillars of Insightful Awareness:

- **Mindfulness (Sati): The Bedrock of Observation:** The very cornerstone of Vipassanā practice is *sati*, a Pali term often rendered in English as mindfulness, bare attention, or simply awareness. It entails the deliberate and sustained act of paying attention to the present moment with a quality of clarity, precision, and unwavering focus, all while maintaining a stance of complete non-judgment. This involves allowing all arising experiences – whether they be thoughts, emotions, physical sensations, or sensory perceptions – to emerge and subsequently pass away without the practitioner becoming entangled in them, reacting to them, or being carried away by their narrative or emotional charge.
- **Non-Judgmental Observation: Witnessing Without Evaluation:** A crucial aspect of Vipassanā is the cultivation of a stance of non-judgmental observation towards all arising experiences. This means observing phenomena precisely as they

manifest, without the habitual tendency to label them as inherently good or bad, pleasant or unpleasant, desirable or undesirable. This deliberate cultivation of non-reactive awareness is a powerful mechanism for breaking deeply ingrained patterns of clinging to what is perceived as pleasant and developing aversion towards what is perceived as unpleasant, patterns that the Buddha identified as the very root of suffering.

- **Present Moment Focus: Anchoring Awareness in the Here and Now:** Vipassanā practice firmly anchors the practitioner's awareness in the immediacy of the present moment, recognizing the fundamental truth that the past is no longer accessible except as a memory, and the future is, as yet, unborn – a realm of mere anticipation and projection. By consistently and gently redirecting the attention back to the unfolding reality of the present, the practitioner gradually frees themselves from the pervasive mental habits of incessant rumination about past events and anxious anticipation of future possibilities, both of which serve as significant sources of mental agitation and suffering.
- **Insight (Vipassanā): The Fruit of Mindful Inquiry:** The very term Vipassanā underscores the ultimate goal of this practice: the arising of profound and transformative insights into the fundamental characteristics of reality – the interconnected truths of impermanence, unsatisfactoriness, and non-self. These insights are not mere intellectual concepts to be grasped through logical deduction or philosophical reasoning. Instead, deep and visceral

experiential realisations emerge organically through sustained and diligent mindful observation. These direct and personal understandings have the potential to dismantle deeply ingrained illusions about the nature of self and reality, leading to profound shifts in perspective and ultimately paving the way for deep and lasting transformation.

Step-by-Step Instructions for a Basic Vipassanā Practice (Mindfulness of Breathing):

1. **Posture: Establishing a Foundation of Stillness and Alertness:** Begin by finding a comfortable and stable posture, allowing for a sense of relaxed alertness. You may choose to sit on a cushion placed on the floor, adopting a cross-legged position, a half-lotus, or a full-lotus posture if these feel natural and sustainable for your body. Alternatively, you can sit upright on a chair with your feet flat on the floor and your back held straight but not rigidly tense, ensuring your spine maintains its natural curvature. Your hands can rest gently in your lap, one palm resting softly in the other, or placed gently on your knees with palms facing upwards or downwards, whichever feels most natural and balanced. Finally, allow your eyes to close gently or to remain softly lowered, directing your gaze downwards and unfocused.

2. **Establishing Awareness of Breath: Anchoring Attention in the Flow of Life:** Gently bring the entirety of your conscious attention to the subtle yet constant sensations of your breath as it naturally enters and leaves your body. You may

become aware of the gentle rising and falling movement of your abdomen with each inhalation and exhalation, the subtle sensation of the air as it passes through your nostrils, perhaps feeling a slight coolness on the inhale and a gentle warmth on the exhale, or the barely perceptible expansion and contraction in your chest area. Choose one specific focus point within this overall experience of breathing that feels most clear and accessible to you, and gently anchor your awareness there, allowing it to become the primary object of your mindful attention.

3. **Observing the Natural Breath: Allowing the Rhythm of Life to Unfold:** Consciously allow your breath to be entirely natural and completely unforced. Refrain from attempting to control, manipulate, or in any way alter its inherent rhythm, depth, or pace. Simply observe the process of inhalation and exhalation precisely as it occurs in each passing moment. Gently notice the beginning of each in-breath, the subtle arc of its middle phase, and the eventual completion of the out-breath. Allow the breath to become a continuous and reliable anchor for your present moment awareness, a constant reminder of the ever-unfolding reality of the here and now.

4. **Dealing with Distractions: The Inevitable Wandering of the Mind:** It is an inherent characteristic of the human mind to wander, to become drawn away from the chosen object of attention by the ceaseless stream of thoughts, emotions, memories, anticipations, sensory perceptions, and a myriad of other mental

phenomena. When you inevitably become aware that your attention has drifted away from the sensations of your breath and become entangled with one of these distractions, gently acknowledge the fact of the distraction itself with a spirit of kindness and complete non-judgment. Avoid becoming frustrated with yourself or criticising your wandering mind. Instead, calmly and with gentle persistence, redirect the focus of your attention back to the primary sensations of your breath. This gentle act of returning your awareness, repeated countless times throughout the course of your meditation session, is in fact the very essence and the core practice of mindfulness.

5. **Expanding Awareness (Optional): Broadening the Scope of Observation:** As your practice deepens and your capacity for sustained attention grows, you may gradually and gently expand the scope of your awareness to encompass other sensations that arise within your physical body, such as subtle feelings of itching, tingling, warmth, or coolness. You may also begin to notice the fleeting presence of various emotions, such as subtle waves of joy, passing moments of sadness, or brief flares of anger. Similarly, you may become aware of the constant stream of thoughts that arise and pass away within the landscape of your mind. When expanding your awareness this way, maintain the same attitude of non-judgmental observation that you cultivate towards the breath. Simply notice these experiences as they arise, acknowledge their presence without getting drawn into their content or narrative, and then gently return the primary focus of

your attention back to your chosen anchor, whether it remains the sensations of your breath or expands to encompass the broader field of your present moment experience.

6. **Duration: Cultivating Consistency Over Intensity:** Begin your practice with shorter meditation sessions, perhaps lasting 10 to 15 minutes. As you become more comfortable with the practice and find that you can sustain your attention with greater ease, you may gradually increase the duration of your sessions. It is important to remember that consistency in your practice, even if it means shorter sessions practised regularly, is often far more beneficial in the long run than infrequent or sporadic longer sessions, especially in the initial stages of cultivating mindfulness.

Variations and Advanced Vipassanā Techniques: Deepening the Practice of Insight:

Beyond the foundational practice of mindfulness of breathing, the Vipassanā tradition encompasses diverse techniques designed to cultivate increasingly refined levels of awareness and deeper insights into the nature of reality. Some of these variations and more advanced techniques include:

- **Body Scan:** This systematic practice involves methodically bringing mindful attention to different body regions, one after the other, noticing any and all sensations that arise in each area without any form of judgment or reaction. This practice cultivates a heightened awareness of the' intricate landscape of bodily sensations and can help release deeply held tension.

- **Walking Meditation:** This practice involves cultivating mindfulness while engaging in the simple act of walking. Practitioners pay close attention to the subtle sensations of each step – the lifting of the foot, the forward movement through space, the placing of the foot on the ground, and the shifting of weight. This integrates mindfulness into movement and can be particularly helpful for those who find sustained sitting challenging.
- **Mindful Movement:** This extends the principle of mindfulness to all forms of physical activity in daily life, such as eating, washing, dressing, or even simply reaching for an object. The focus is on bringing conscious awareness to the sensations and intentions behind each movement, breaking free from habitual autopilot.
- **Noting Practice:** This technique involves mentally labelling experiences as they arise. For example, if you notice a thought, you might silently label it as "thinking." If you feel an emotion, you might label it as "feeling." If you hear a sound, you might label it as "hearing." This precise mental noting can enhance clarity, sharpen awareness, and foster a greater sense of detachment from the constant flow of experience.

Benefits and Potential Challenges of Vipassanā: Navigating the Path of Insight:

The consistent and dedicated practice of Vipassanā meditation can lead to a wide array of significant benefits, including a noticeable reduction in stress and anxiety levels, a marked increase in self-awareness and understanding, improved concentration and focus, greater emotional regulation and resilience, and the gradual development of profound and transformative insights into the fundamental nature of reality. However, it is also important to acknowledge that practitioners may encounter certain challenges along the path. These can include periods of restlessness and agitation, feelings of boredom or dullness, the surfacing of uncomfortable or suppressed emotions, or the unexpected arising of difficult memories. It is crucial to approach these challenges with patience, acceptance, and a spirit of gentle curiosity. Seeking guidance from experienced and qualified Vipassanā teachers can be immensely helpful in navigating these difficulties and deepening one's practice.

Samatha-Bhāvanā (Concentration Meditation): Cultivating the Stillness of a Focused Mind:

Samatha-Bhāvanā, often translated as "tranquillity development," "concentration cultivation," or "calm abiding," represents another essential category of Buddhist meditation practices. Unlike Vipassanā's focus on insight through mindful observation, Samatha-Bhāvanā centres on the deliberate training of the mind to become progressively still, deeply focused, and unified in its attention on a single, chosen object. The primary aim of this practice is to cultivate mental stability (*samadhi*) and to foster a profound state of inner calm, clarity, and unwavering focus. While Samatha can be practised as an end in itself, leading to deep states of relaxation and mental clarity, it is also frequently viewed within the Buddhist tradition as a crucial and foundational prerequisite for the deeper penetrative insights that arise from Vipassanā practice. A mind that has been calmed and rendered more focused through Samatha is considered far better equipped to observe reality's subtle nuances with clarity and penetrate its true nature.

Core Principles of Samatha-Bhāvanā: The Foundations of Focused Tranquillity:

- **Single-Pointed Concentration (Ekaggata):** The fundamental aim of Samatha practice is to intentionally direct and then sustain the entirety of one's attentional focus on a carefully chosen single object, without allowing the mind to waver, become distracted, or become entangled in the myriad of other mental phenomena that may arise.
- **Sustained Attention: The Cultivation of Mental Endurance:** Samatha involves the gradual and persistent training of the mind to remain steadily and continuously focused on the chosen object of attention for increasingly longer periods of time, thereby developing mental stamina and the capacity for sustained concentration.
- **Mental Clarity: The Stillness that Reveals:** As the practitioner's concentration deepens and becomes more stable, the mind naturally becomes clearer, less cluttered with the incessant stream of discursive thoughts, and increasingly present and receptive to the subtle nuances of experience.
- **Tranquillity (Samatha): The Fruit of Focused Abiding:** The consistent and dedicated practice of Samatha ultimately cultivates a profound

sense of inner peace, deep stillness, and an abiding feeling of well-being that arises from a mind that is no longer constantly agitated and scattered.

Common Objects of Concentration in Samatha Practice: Anchors for the Focused Mind:

The Samatha tradition utilises various objects as anchors for the mind's focus. Some of the most common include:

- **The Breath:** Similar to its use in Vipassanā, the breath can be a primary object of concentration in Samatha. However, the emphasis here is less on analysing the breath's characteristics and more on sustaining unwavering attention on the sensation of breathing itself at a chosen point, such as the nostrils or the abdomen.
- **Mantra:** The focused and rhythmic repetition of a specific word, phrase, or sacred sound (mantra) can be a powerful tool for quieting mental chatter and directing the mind's attention to a single point.
- **Visualisations: Concentrating on a specific mental image, such as a particular colour**, a meaningful symbol, or the form of a deity, can effectively focus the mind and cultivate inner stillness.
- **Kasinas:** These are traditional objects of concentration, often involving focusing on a physical disc or element, such as a disc of earth, water, fire, air, or coloured material.

Step-by-Step Instructions for a Basic Samatha Practice (Breath Concentration):

1. **Posture:** Adopt a comfortable and stable sitting posture, similar to the guidelines provided for Vipassanā practice.
2. **Choosing the Object:** Gently bring your attention to the sensation of your breath. Select one specific point of focus, such as the feeling of the air entering and leaving your nostrils, the gentle rising and falling of your abdomen, or the subtle sensation at the tip of your nose and commit to keeping your attention anchored at this chosen point for the duration of your meditation session.
3. **Sustaining Attention: Gentle Persistence:** Gently but firmly direct your attention to your chosen point of focus on the breath. When you inevitably notice that your mind has wandered (as it naturally will), simply acknowledge the distraction with a spirit of non-judgment and then patiently and lovingly bring your attention back to the chosen sensation of the breath.
4. **Working with Distractions: The Practice of Returning:** Recognise that distractions are an inherent and unavoidable part of training the mind. Avoid becoming frustrated or discouraged when your attention drifts. Simply recognize that your mind has wandered, and then gently and kindly redirect it back to the anchor of your breath. The very act of repeatedly returning your attention is the core of the practice.
5. **Counting the Breath (Optional): A Tool for Focus:** To aid in maintaining focus, particularly in

the initial stages of practice, you may find it helpful to count your breaths silently. For example, you might silently count "in, one; out, one; in, two; out, two," and so on, up to a count of ten, and then gently begin the counting cycle again at one. If you notice that your mind wanders away from the breath and the counting before you reach ten, simply return your attention to the beginning of the counting cycle.

6. **Observing the Qualities of Breath (Advanced): Refining Awareness:** As your concentration deepens and becomes more stable, you may begin to notice increasingly subtle qualities of the breath, such as its relative length (long or short), its temperature (warm or cool), or the subtle sensations it creates in different parts of your body. Simply observe these nuances without attempting to change or manipulate the breath.

7. **Duration:** Begin with shorter meditation sessions, perhaps lasting for 10 to 15 minutes, and gradually increase the duration as your ability to sustain focus improves. Regularity of practice is far more important than the length of individual sessions, especially in developing concentration.

Stages of Samadhi (Absorption): The Deepening of Mental Stillness:

In the more advanced stages of Samatha practice, practitioners may experience progressively deeper mental absorption states, traditionally known as *jhanas*. These profound states are characterised by increasingly heightened levels of tranquillity, intense joy, and unwavering concentration, often accompanied by a noticeable diminishing of sensory input from the external world and a significant quieting of discursive thought. While the attainment of the jhanas is not necessarily the primary goal of all Buddhist meditation

Meditation Journey

Chapter 3: The Hindu Traditions of Meditation: A Multifaceted Path to Inner Realisation

The ancient and profoundly rich tapestry of Hinduism, far from being a monolithic entity, encompasses a vast and diverse spectrum of philosophical schools, theological perspectives, and an intricate array of spiritual practices. Within this expansive and enduring tradition, meditation, or *dhyana* as it is often referred to, holds a position of paramount importance as a fundamental pathway to achieving profound inner realisation, transcending the limitations of the ego, and ultimately realising the inherent unity of the individual soul (*Atman*) with the ultimate, all-pervading reality (*Brahman*). Unlike the more unified approach often associated with early Buddhism, Hindu meditation practices are as varied and multifaceted as the tradition, reflecting the diverse temperaments, philosophical inclinations, and specific deities or paths emphasised by its numerous schools and lineages. This chapter will delve into a more detailed exploration of some key Hindu meditation traditions, meticulously examining their historical context, carefully outlining their core principles and techniques, and providing more comprehensive guidance for engaging in these diverse and transformative practices.

The Foundational Role of Yoga: Patanjali's Eight Limbs and the Path to Raja Yoga

As briefly introduced in Chapter 1, the classical system of Yoga, most systematically codified in the Yoga Sutras of Patanjali (likely compiled between the 2nd century BCE and the 4th century CE), stands as one of the most influential and comprehensive frameworks for meditation within the Hindu tradition. Patanjali's Yoga is often referred to as *Raja Yoga*, the "royal path" to self-realisation, and it meticulously outlines an eight-limbed path (*ashtanga*) that serves as a progressive and holistic guide to achieving the ultimate state of meditative absorption and liberation. While the physical postures (*asanas*) and breath control practices (*pranayama*) are perhaps the most widely recognised aspects of Yoga in the modern West, they constitute only the initial stages of Patanjali's comprehensive system, serving as essential preparatory steps for the deeper and more transformative practices of meditation.

Patanjali's Eight Limbs of Yoga and Their Relation to Meditation:

1. **Yamas (Ethical Restraints):** These five ethical principles—nonviolence (ahimsa), truthfulness (satya), non-stealing (asteya), celibacy/continence (brahmacharya), and non-possessiveness (aparigraha)—form the moral and ethical foundation for a meaningful spiritual practice. Cultivating these restraints purifies the

mind and reduces the internal conflict hindering meditative progress.

2. **Niyamas (Observances):** These five positive observances – purity (*shaucha*), contentment (*santosha*), austerity/self-discipline (*tapas*), self-study (*svadhyaya*), and devotion to a higher power (*ishvara pranidhana*) – further refine the practitioner's inner landscape, fostering qualities conducive to deeper concentration and insight.

3. **Asana (Physical Postures):** The practice of steady and comfortable physical postures aims to cultivate physical stability, strength, and flexibility, thereby reducing physical distractions and allowing the body to remain still for extended periods of meditation.

4. **Pranayama (Breath Control):** The conscious regulation of breath is considered a vital link between the body and the mind. Various breathing techniques are employed to calm the nervous system, balance energy flow, and prepare the mind for deeper states of concentration.

5. **Pratyahara (Withdrawal of the Senses):** This crucial limb involves intentionally drawing the senses inward, detaching awareness from external stimuli. This inward focus reduces external distractions and allows the practitioner to turn their attention towards the inner world.

6. **Dharana (Concentration):** This is the initial stage of formal meditation, involving the focused concentration of the mind on a single point of attention. This object can be an external object (like a candle flame or a deity image), an internal sensation (like the breath or the heart chakra), or a

mental concept. The aim is to sustain unbroken attention on this chosen object.

7. **Dhyana (Meditation):** This is the deepening of *dharana*. When concentration becomes sustained, effortless, and unbroken, it evolves into meditation. In *dhyana*, the distinction between the observer and the observed begins to blur, and a state of deep absorption arises.

8. **Samadhi (Union/Liberation):** This is the ultimate aim of Raja Yoga, a state of profound union with the object of meditation, transcending the individual self and realising the interconnectedness with the ultimate reality. *Samadhi* is characterised by deep peace, bliss, and a profound understanding of the true nature of reality.

Step-by-Step Instructions for a Basic Raja Yoga Meditation (Focus on Breath):

1. **Preparation:** Find a quiet and comfortable space where you will not be disturbed. Sit in a steady and comfortable posture (*asana*), such as Padmasana (Lotus Pose), Sukhasana (Easy Pose), or even seated comfortably in a chair with a straight spine. Close your eyes gently.

2. **Ethical Foundation:** Bring to mind the Yamas and Niyamas, consciously aligning your intention with these ethical principles and positive observances.

3. **Pranayama (Optional):** You can begin with a few rounds of gentle breath control exercises, such as Ujjayi breath (Ocean Breath) or Nadi Shodhana

(Alternate Nostril Breathing), to calm the nervous system and focus the mind.

4. **Pratyahara (Sense Withdrawal):** Gently draw your senses inward, releasing your attention from external sights, sounds, and sensations. Turn your awareness towards your inner experience.

5. **Dharana (Concentration on Breath):** Bring your attention to the natural flow of your breath. Choose a specific point of focus, such as the sensation of the breath entering and leaving your nostrils or the gentle rise and fall of your abdomen. Sustain your attention on this point without judgment. When your mind wanders (as it will), gently and patiently bring it back to your breath.

6. **Dhyana (Meditation):** As your concentration deepens and becomes more sustained and effortless, allow yourself to rest in this awareness of the breath. The distinction between your awareness and the sensation of breath may begin to soften. Remain present and allow the experience to unfold naturally without striving or forcing.

7. **Duration:** Begin with shorter sessions of 10-15 minutes and gradually increase the duration as your capacity for sustained concentration develops.

Bhakti Yoga: The Path of Devotion and Surrender Through Meditation

Bhakti Yoga, the yoga of devotion, offers a profoundly different yet equally powerful approach to meditation within the Hindu tradition. Instead of focusing primarily on intellectual understanding or rigorous mental discipline, Bhakti Yoga emphasises intense love, devotion, and surrender towards a chosen deity or the divine. Meditation in Bhakti Yoga often takes the form of focused contemplation on the attributes, stories, and forms of the beloved deity, aiming to establish a deep emotional connection and ultimately experience a profound union with the divine through love.

Key Practices in Bhakti Yoga Meditation:

- **Mantra Japa:** The repetitive recitation of sacred names, hymns, or mantras dedicated to the chosen deity. This practice focuses the mind, purifies the heart, and evokes feelings of devotion.
- **Kirtan and Bhajan:** Devotional singing and chanting of sacred songs and hymns, often accompanied by music, creates a powerful emotional and communal experience of devotion.
- **Puja (Worship):** Ritualistic offerings and worship performed to the deity, often involving specific gestures, prayers, and visualizations. This practice cultivates a tangible connection with the divine.
- **Visualisation of the Divine Form:** Focusing the mind on the beautiful and inspiring form of the chosen deity, contemplating its attributes and symbolic meanings.
- **Storytelling (Katha):** Listening to and reflecting upon the sacred stories and legends of the deity, deepening one's understanding and love.
- **Surrender (Sharanagati):** The ultimate act of Bhakti, involving a complete and heartfelt surrender of the ego and all actions to the will of the divine.

Lawrence Finch

Step-by-Step Instructions for a Basic Bhakti Yoga Meditation (Mantra Japa):

1. **Preparation:** Find a quiet and sacred space. You may wish to have an image or symbol of your chosen deity present. Sit comfortably with a straight spine.
2. **Invocation:** Begin by praying or invoking your chosen deity, expressing your love and devotion.
3. **Choosing a Mantra:** Select a mantra that is sacred to your chosen deity and resonates with your heart. Common mantras include "Om Namah Shivaya" (to Shiva), "Om Namo Narayanaya" (to Vishnu), or "Om Shri Krishnaya Namaha" (to Krishna).
4. **Recitation:** Begin to gently and rhythmically recite the mantra. You can do this aloud or silently. You can use a *mala* (prayer beads) to keep track of the repetitions.
5. **Focus and Devotion:** As you recite the mantra, focus on the sound and the meaning of the words. Cultivate feelings of love, devotion, and connection with your chosen deity. Allow your heart to open.
6. **Visualisation (Optional): You can also visualise** the form of your deity as you recite the mantra, focusing on its beauty and divine qualities.
7. **Surrender:** At the end of your practice, offer a prayer of surrender, releasing any expectations or desires and offering your devotion to the divine.
8. **Duration:** Practice for a period that feels meaningful to you, starting with 10-15 minutes and gradually increasing as desired.

Jnana Yoga: The Path of Wisdom and Self-Inquiry Through Meditation

Jnana Yoga, the yoga of wisdom or knowledge, takes a more intellectual and introspective approach to meditation. It emphasizes the power of discrimination (*viveka*) between the real (Brahman) and the unreal (the illusory world of *maya*), and the direct inquiry into the true nature of the Self (*Atman*) through rigorous self-analysis and contemplation of profound philosophical truths. Meditation in Jnana Yoga often involves deep contemplation on Vedantic teachings and the systematic dismantling of false identifications with the body, mind, and ego.

Key Practices in Jnana Yoga Meditation:

- **Shravana (Hearing):** Studying and listening to enlightened teachers' teachings and the wisdom of the scriptures (Upanishads, Brahma Sutras, Bhagavad Gita).
- **Manana (Reflection):** Deeply reflecting upon and contemplating the meaning of these teachings, assimilating them intellectually.
- **Nididhyasana (Contemplation):** Sustained and profound contemplation on the nature of the Self and the ultimate reality, aiming for direct experiential understanding. This often involves self-inquiry practices like "Who am I?" (*Atma-vichara*).
- **Neti-Neti (Not This, Not That):** A process of mentally negating all that is not the true Self – the body, senses, mind, intellect, ego – to arrive at the pure, underlying consciousness.

Step-by-Step Instructions for a Basic Jnana Yoga Meditation (Self-Inquiry - "Who am I?"):

1. **Preparation:** Find a quiet and comfortable space. Sit with a straight spine.
2. **Intention:** Set the intention to inquire into the true nature of your Self.
3. **The Question:** Ask yourself, "Who am I?"
4. **Observe Arising Identifications:** As thoughts and identifications arise (e.g., "I am my body," "I am my thoughts," "I am my emotions," "I am my job"), systematically negate each one with "Neti, Neti" – "Not this, not this."
5. **Stay with the Feeling of "I":** After negating these false identifications, remain with the fundamental feeling of "I" that persists. Explore this feeling directly. What is its source? What is its nature?
6. **Sustain Inquiry:** Continue to gently and persistently inquire into the nature of this "I" without seeking intellectual answers. Allow direct experiential understanding to arise.
7. **Rest in Awareness:** As you delve deeper, you may experience moments of stillness and pure awareness beyond the limitations of the ego. Rest in this awareness.
8. **Duration:** Practice for a period conducive to deep contemplation, starting with 15-20 minutes or longer.

Karma Yoga: The Path of Selfless Action Through Mindful Engagement

Karma Yoga, the yoga of selfless action, offers a unique approach to meditation by emphasising the importance of performing all actions with detachment, without attachment to the results, and with a spirit of service to a higher purpose or the divine. When done with mindful awareness, equanimity, and a focus on the present moment, the very act of engaging in work and daily life becomes a form of meditation.

Key Principles of Karma Yoga Meditation:

- **Action Without Attachment:** Performing duties and responsibilities without craving specific outcomes or fearing negative results.
- **Equanimity:** Maintaining a balanced and even-minded attitude towards success and failure, praise and blame.
- **Selfless Service:** Dedicating one's actions to a higher cause or the well-being of others, without expectation of personal reward.
- **Mindful Presence in Action:** Bringing full awareness and concentration to the task, fully engaging in the present moment of action.

Integrating Karma Yoga into Daily Life as Meditation:

- **Set an Intention:** Before undertaking any task, intend to perform it with mindfulness and without attachment to the outcome.

- **Focus on the Process:** Bring your full attention to the steps involved in the action, rather than solely focusing on the end result.
- **Observe Your Reactions:** As you work, notice your thoughts and emotions, maintaining a detached and equanimous perspective.
- **Offer Your Actions:** Mentally offer the fruits of your labour to a higher power or the benefit of all beings.
- **Find Joy in the Doing:** Cultivate a sense of joy and engagement in the present moment of action, regardless of the task.

The Interconnectedness of Hindu Meditation Traditions

While these four major paths of Yoga (Raja, Bhakti, Jnana, and Karma) offer distinct approaches to meditation, it is important to recognise that in practice, they often intertwine and complement one another. A Bhakti Yogi may engage in mantra japa with focused concentration (Raja Yoga), while a Jnana Yogi may cultivate deep devotion (Bhakti Yoga) as part of their practice. The ultimate goal across these diverse traditions remains the same: the realisation of the true Self and its inherent unity with the divine, achieved through the transformative power of a disciplined and focused mind. The multifaceted nature of Hindu meditation reflects the diverse paths that individuals may take on their journey towards inner realisation, honouring each seeker's unique temperaments and inclinations.

Meditation Journey

Chapter 4: Beyond India: The Meditative Landscapes of Jainism and Other Eastern Traditions

While the Indian subcontinent served as the primary crucible for the systematic development and profound articulation of many core meditative practices, the human impulse towards inner exploration and the cultivation of heightened awareness was not confined to its geographical boundaries. Across Asia's vast and diverse tapestry, other ancient traditions independently developed or significantly adapted contemplative practices that shared fundamental aims with their Indian counterparts – the quieting of the mind, the cultivation of insight, and the pursuit of inner peace or liberation. This chapter will delve into a more detailed examination of the meditative traditions within Jainism, which shares a close historical and philosophical relationship with early Indian thought, and then broaden our scope to explore the unique and influential contemplative practices that emerged in other significant Eastern traditions, including Taoism and Confucianism in China, and the distinct meditative approaches found within the spiritual landscape of Japan.

Jainism: The Rigorous Path of Self-Discipline and Meditation for Liberation

As introduced in Chapter 3, Jainism, an ancient Indian religion that arose around the same time as early Buddhism, places an exceptionally strong emphasis on the practice of meditation as a crucial and indispensable means for the purification of the soul (*jiva*) from the accumulated burden of karmic matter and the ultimate attainment of liberation (*moksha*). Jain philosophy posits that the soul is inherently pure, possessing infinite knowledge, bliss, and power. Still, these intrinsic qualities are obscured by karma's constant influx and attachment, conceived as a subtle, physical substance resulting from one's thoughts, words, and deeds. Meditation in Jainism is therefore not merely a mental exercise. Still, a rigorous and transformative practice aimed at diligently stopping the influx of new karma (*samvara*) and systematically shedding the karma that has already accumulated (*nirjara*), thereby progressively unveiling the soul's pristine and luminous nature.

Key Meditative Practices in Jainism:

- **Samayika (Equanimity Practice):** This is a foundational Jain practice involving dedicated periods (often 48 minutes) spent cultivating equanimity, introspection, and detachment from worldly concerns. During *Samayika*, practitioners often engage in scriptural study, silent reflection on Jain principles, and various forms of mental concentration. It is a crucial daily discipline for fostering inner balance and reducing karmic attachment.

- **Dhyana (Concentration and Contemplation):** Jain texts describe various forms of *Dhyana*, encompassing both focused concentration on a single object and deeper contemplation on core Jain principles such as the nature of the soul, the causes of suffering, and the path to liberation. Specific forms of *Dhyana* include focusing on the inherent qualities of the soul, reflecting on the impermanent nature of the body and worldly possessions, and contemplating the interconnectedness of all living beings.

- **Kayotsarga (Body Abandonment):** This unique Jain practice involves standing or lying motionless for extended periods, often in specific postures, with a complete detachment from the physical body. *Kayotsarga* is not merely a physical endurance exercise, but a powerful meditative discipline aimed at transcending attachment to the body, cultivating mental steadfastness, and allowing karmic impurities to be shed.

- **Preksha Dhyana (Perception Meditation):** A more contemporary yet deeply rooted Jain meditation system developed in the 20th century, *Preksha Dhyana* focuses on consciously observing and regulating one's breath, thoughts, emotions, and subtle energy centres within the body. It incorporates techniques for purifying mental and emotional states, developing self-awareness, and experiencing inner peace. *Preksha Dhyana* emphasises a systematic approach to self-transformation through mindful observation and regulation of internal processes.

- **Mantra Recitation:** Similar to Hindu traditions, the recitation of specific Jain mantras, often dedicated to the Tirthankaras (the enlightened spiritual teachers of Jainism), is also practised as a form of focused meditation to purify the mind and cultivate devotion.

Step-by-Step Instructions for a Basic Jain Meditation (Samayika - Focused Reflection):

1. **Preparation:** Find a clean and quiet space. Sit comfortably in a stable posture, such as Padmasana, Ardha-Padmasana (Half-Lotus), or Sukhasana. You can also sit upright on a chair if needed.
2. **Intention Setting:** Begin by setting a clear intention for your *Samayika* period, resolving to remain composed, engage in introspection, and detach from external distractions.
3. **Posture and Stillness:** Maintain a steady and motionless posture throughout the practice. This physical stillness aids in cultivating mental stillness.
4. **Focused Reflection:** Choose a specific Jain principle or teaching to reflect upon deeply. This could be the nature of non-violence (*ahimsa*), the concept of karma, the soul's qualities, or the Tirthankaras' teachings. Gently guide your mind to contemplate the meaning and implications of this principle in your own life.
5. **Breath Awareness:** You can gently bring your awareness to the natural flow of your breath as an

anchor for your attention, returning to it whenever your mind wanders.

6. **Non-Attachment:** Consciously cultivate a state of non-attachment towards any thoughts or emotions that may arise during your *Samayika*. Observe them without judgment and allow them to pass without engaging with them.

7. **Mantra Recitation (Optional):** You may silently or softly recite a Jain mantra, such as "Om Arham," to focus your mind and generate positive vibrations.

8. **Concluding the Practice:** At the end of the designated time, gradually release your focus and gently bring your awareness back to your surroundings, whilst feeling serene.

9. **Duration:** Traditionally, *Samayika* lasts 48 minutes, but you can begin with shorter durations and gradually increase the time as your practice deepens.

Taoism: The Flow of the Tao and the Cultivation of Inner Harmony

Emerging from ancient China, Taoism, a profound philosophical and spiritual tradition attributed to Lao Tzu (around the 6th century BCE), offers a unique perspective on inner cultivation and the attainment of harmony with the natural order of the universe, known as the Tao (the Way). While not always explicitly labelled as "meditation" in the same way as Indian traditions, Taoism encompasses a rich array of contemplative practices aimed at quieting the mind, cultivating inner stillness, and aligning oneself with the effortless flow of the Tao.

Key Contemplative Practices in Taoism:

- **Zuo Wang (Sitting in Oblivion):** This practice involves transcending the limitations of the intellect and conceptual thought, entering a state of deep stillness and emptiness where one can directly experience the underlying unity of all things. It is a profound form of non-doing (*wu wei*) applied to the mind.
- **Nei Guan (Inner Observation):** This involves a focused and sustained inward gaze, observing the subtle movements of energy (*Qi*), the interplay of emotions, and the arising of thoughts without judgment or engagement. It is a process of becoming intimately familiar with one's inner landscape.
- **Cun Si (Focused Thought/Visualisation): This practice involves directing focused intention and visualisation towards specific energy centres** (*dantian*) or internal processes to cultivate and circulate *Qi* within the body. It can also involve visualising harmonious natural imagery to align oneself with the Tao.
- **Qigong and Tai Chi:** These gentle movement practices, deeply rooted in Taoist principles, can be considered forms of "meditation in motion." They involve slow, deliberate movements synchronised with breath to cultivate and balance *Qi*, promote physical health, and foster a mindful presence.
- **Breathwork (Tu Na):** Various Taoist breathing techniques aim to regulate the flow of *Qi*, calm the mind, and enhance vitality. These practices often

involve specific rhythms, depths, and retentions of breath.

Step-by-Step Instructions for a Basic Taoist Contemplation (Breath and Lower Dantian):

1. **Preparation:** Find a quiet and comfortable space. Sit upright in a chair with your feet flat on the floor or cross-legged on a cushion. Relax your shoulders and allow your hands to rest gently in your lap.
2. **Centring:** Gently bring awareness to your lower dantian, about two inches below your navel and one inch inward. This is considered a primary centre of energy in the body.
3. **Natural Breathing:** Become aware of your natural breath flowing in and out of your body. Do not try to control it; simply observe its rhythm and depth.
4. **Following the Breath to the Dantian:** Gently guide your awareness down to your lower dantian with each inhale. With each exhale, allow your awareness to rest there. Imagine the breath gently filling and emptying this energy centre.
5. **Cultivating Stillness:** As you continue to focus on your breath and the lower *dantian*, allow your mind to become increasingly still. Release any thoughts or distractions that arise without judgment, gently returning your focus to your breath and the *dantian*.
6. **Visualisation (Optional): You can gently visualise** a soft, warm glow or a feeling of gentle

energy accumulating in your lower *dantian* with each breath.

7. **Duration:** Begin with sessions of 10-15 minutes and gradually increase the duration as you feel comfortable.

Confucianism: Cultivating Virtue and Social Harmony Through Self-Discipline

While Confucianism, founded by Confucius (around 5th century BCE) in China, is primarily known as a system of ethics, social harmony, and good governance, it also emphasises the critical importance of self-cultivation and rigorous mental discipline as foundational to becoming a virtuous individual and a contributing member of society. Although not always framed as "meditation" in the same way as other traditions, the Confucian emphasis on introspection, self-reflection, and the cultivation of inner stillness significantly overlaps with the aims of contemplative practices.

Contemplative Aspects of Confucianism:

- **Self-Reflection (省 - Xǐng):** Confucian teachings strongly encourage regular and deep self-reflection on one's thoughts, words, and actions, examining whether they align with the principles of *ren* (benevolence, humaneness), *li* (ritual propriety), and *yi* (righteousness). This introspective process cultivates self-awareness and promotes moral development.
- **Quiet Sitting (靜坐 - Jìngzuò):** While not as elaborately developed as in other traditions, the

practice of quiet sitting was recognised within Confucianism as a means to cultivate mental stillness, focus the mind, and enhance concentration, which were seen as essential for learning and moral cultivation.

- **Study and Contemplation of Classics:** The rigorous study and deep contemplation of the Confucian classics were considered a form of mental discipline that fostered wisdom, understanding, and the internalization of virtuous principles.
- **Ritual Practice (禮 - Lǐ):** Rituals' mindful and sincere performance was seen as a way to cultivate inner harmony, respect, and a sense of connection to tradition and community. Focusing on proper conduct and intention during rituals required a degree of mental presence.

A Simple Confucian Practice of Self-Reflection:

1. **Preparation:** Find a quiet time and space to reflect without interruption. Sit comfortably.
2. **Focus on a Virtue:** Choose one of the core Confucian virtues, such as *ren* (benevolence), *li* (propriety), or *zhi* (wisdom).
3. **Introspective Inquiry:** Reflect on your actions, thoughts, and words from the past day (or a longer period). Ask yourself:
    - In what ways did I embody this virtue?
    - In what ways did I fall short?
    - What were the underlying motivations behind my actions and thoughts?

Meditation Journey
- What can I learn from these reflections to better cultivate this virtue in the future?
4. **Journaling (Optional):** You may find it helpful to write down your reflections to gain greater clarity and track your progress.
5. **Setting Intention:** Conclude by setting a clear intention for how you will strive to embody the chosen virtue in your actions and thoughts going forward.

Japanese Traditions: Zen and the Art of Mindful Presence

In Japan, Buddhism's arrival and subsequent flourishing, particularly the Zen (Chan) school, led to the development of unique and influential meditative practices deeply integrated into Japanese culture and aesthetics. Zen emphasizes direct experience and intuitive understanding, often bypassing intellectual analysis in pursuing enlightenment (*satori*).

Key Meditative Practices in Zen Buddhism:

- **Zazen (Seated Meditation):** This is the central practice of Zen. It involves sitting in a specific posture (often cross-legged on a cushion) with a straight spine and a focused yet open awareness. The emphasis is on simply being present with whatever arises without judgment or interference.
- **Koan Practice:** Koans are paradoxical riddles or enigmatic statements designed to break down

habitual thought patterns and logic, leading to sudden flashes of insight. Contemplating koans is a central meditative practice in Rinzai Zen.

- **Shikantaza (Just Sitting):** This more subtle practice, emphasized in Soto Zen, involves simply sitting with no specific object of focus, cultivating a state of wide-open awareness of the present moment.
- **Mindful Movement (Kinhin):** Walking meditation practised slowly and deliberately, maintaining awareness of each step.
- **Integration into Arts:** Zen principles of mindfulness and presence are often integrated into traditional Japanese arts such as calligraphy (Shodo), tea ceremony (Chanoyu), flower arrangement (Ikebana), and martial arts (like Aikido and Kyudo), transforming these activities into forms of moving meditation.

Step-by-Step Instructions for Basic Zazen (Seated Meditation):

1. **Posture:** Sit on a firm cushion (zafu) on a flat surface. Adopt a stable posture, such as the full lotus, half-lotus, Burmese position, or simply cross-legged. If these are uncomfortable, you can sit on a chair with your feet flat on the floor. Maintain a straight but relaxed spine, with your ears aligned over your shoulders and your nose aligned with your navel.
2. **Hand Position (Mudra):** Place your hands in the cosmic mudra (hosshinkai-join): your right hand rests palm-up in your lap, and your left hand rests

palm-up on top of your right, with the tips of your thumbs lightly touching, forming an oval.

3. **Eyes:** Your eyes can be gently closed or slightly open, and your soft, unfocused gaze can be directed downwards about two to three feet in front of you.

4. **Breath:** Bring your awareness to your breath. Allow it to flow naturally and without any control. Simply observe the sensation of the breath as it enters and leaves your body, perhaps at your nostrils or in your abdomen.

5. **Awareness:** Be aware of whatever arises – thoughts, feelings, sensations, sounds. Do not grasp onto them, judge them, or try to change them. Simply acknowledge their presence and allow them to pass, like clouds drifting across the sky.

6. **Returning:** When your mind wanders (as it inevitably will), gently and without self-criticism, bring your awareness back to your breath or the simple act of being present.

7. **Duration:** Begin with short sessions of 5-10 minutes and gradually increase the duration as you become more comfortable.

The meditative landscapes beyond India reveal a rich and diverse array of contemplative practices, each shaped by unique cultural and philosophical contexts yet sharing the fundamental human aspiration for inner peace, self-understanding, and a deeper connection to the nature of reality. From the rigorous self-discipline of Jain meditation to the harmonious flow of Taoist contemplation and the direct experiential focus of Zen, these traditions offer invaluable insights into the multifaceted ways humanity

Lawrence Finch
has sought to cultivate the inner life and unlock the transformative potential of the human mind.

Meditation Journey

Chapter 5: The Rise of Secular Mindfulness: Bridging Ancient Wisdom and Modern Science

While the roots of mindfulness are undeniably embedded in the rich soil of ancient Eastern contemplative traditions, particularly within Buddhism, the latter half of the 20th century witnessed a significant and transformative phenomenon: the emergence and rapid growth of secular mindfulness. This movement involved extracting mindfulness's core principles and practices from their traditional religious and philosophical contexts and adapting them into evidence-based interventions applicable across various secular settings, including healthcare, psychology, education, and the workplace. This chapter will delve into the key figures and pivotal developments that led to the rise of secular mindfulness, meticulously examine its core principles and techniques as they are applied in contemporary contexts, and explore the diverse and impactful applications of these practices in addressing various modern challenges and promoting well-being.

Key Figures and Foundational Developments in Secular Mindfulness:

The translation and adaptation of Buddhist mindfulness practices into secular frameworks was not a sudden occurrence but rather a gradual process influenced by several key individuals and converging trends:

- **The Influence of Buddhist Scholars and Teachers:** The increasing interaction between Western scholars, psychologists, and Buddhist teachers in the mid-20th century played a crucial role in introducing the core concepts of mindfulness to a Western audience. Figures like Thich Nhat Hanh, a Vietnamese Zen Buddhist monk and peace activist, and Shunryu Suzuki Roshi, a Japanese Soto Zen monk who founded the San Francisco Zen Centre, were instrumental in demystifying mindfulness and highlighting its potential for cultivating inner peace and reducing suffering in a way that resonated with Western sensibilities. Their writings and teachings emphasised the practical application of mindfulness in everyday life.
- **Early Explorations in Psychology and Therapy:** Pioneering psychologists began to explore the potential of incorporating mindfulness principles into therapeutic approaches. Carl Rogers' emphasis on present-moment awareness in client-centred therapy and Steven Hayes' development of Acceptance and Commitment Therapy (ACT), which utilises acceptance and mindfulness strategies to promote psychological flexibility, laid some of the early groundwork for the more explicit integration of mindfulness.
- **Jon Kabat-Zinn and Mindfulness-Based Stress Reduction (MBSR):** Arguably the most pivotal figure in the popularization of secular mindfulness is Dr. Jon Kabat-Zinn, a molecular

biologist who, in 1979, founded the Stress Reduction Clinic at the University of Massachusetts Medical School. Kabat-Zinn meticulously adapted core Buddhist mindfulness meditation practices into a structured, eight-week program called Mindfulness-Based Stress Reduction (MBSR). Crucially, MBSR presented mindfulness in a clear, secular, and scientifically rigorous framework, focusing on its potential to alleviate stress, chronic pain, anxiety, and depression without explicit religious or philosophical underpinnings. The rigorous research conducted on the efficacy of MBSR in clinical settings provided the crucial scientific validation that propelled the widespread adoption of secular mindfulness.

- **Mark Williams, John Teasdale, and Mindfulness-Based Cognitive Therapy (MBCT):** Building upon the success of MBSR, clinical psychologists Mark Williams, John Teasdale, and Zindel Segal adapted mindfulness practices specifically for the prevention of relapse in recurrent depression. Their eight-week Mindfulness-Based Cognitive Therapy (MBCT) program integrated core mindfulness meditation techniques with principles of cognitive behavioural therapy (CBT) to help individuals become more aware of and disengage from negative thought patterns that can trigger depressive episodes. The strong empirical evidence supporting the effectiveness of MBCT further solidified the credibility and widespread adoption of secular mindfulness in mental healthcare.

Core Principles and Techniques of Secular Mindfulness:

While drawing heavily from traditional Buddhist practices, secular mindfulness emphasises the practical application of these principles in a way that is accessible and relevant to individuals from all backgrounds, regardless of their religious or spiritual beliefs. The core principles and techniques commonly employed in secular mindfulness interventions include:

- **Present Moment Awareness:** At its heart, secular mindfulness involves intentional and nonjudgmental attention to the present moment—to thoughts, feelings, bodily sensations, and sensory experiences as they arise and pass away. The focus is on cultivating a direct and immediate awareness of "what is" without being carried away by rumination about the past or worrying about the future.
- **Non-Judgmental Acceptance:** A crucial element of secular mindfulness is cultivating a non-reactive and accepting attitude towards all experiences, whether they are perceived as pleasant, unpleasant, or neutral. This involves observing thoughts and feelings without labelling them as "good" or "bad" or trying to suppress or change them. The emphasis is on allowing experiences to be as they are.
- **Attention to the Breath:** The breath is often used as a primary anchor for attention in secular mindfulness practices. Its continuous and ever-present nature makes it a readily available and

reliable point of focus for cultivating present-moment awareness.

- **Body Scan Meditation:** This technique systematically brings mindful attention to different body parts, noticing any sensations that arise without judgment. It helps to cultivate body awareness and can be particularly helpful in addressing chronic pain and physical tension.
- **Mindful Movement:** Drawing inspiration from practices like walking meditation and mindful yoga, secular mindfulness incorporates mindful movement exercises that bring conscious awareness to the physical sensations of movement in everyday activities.
- **Mindful Awareness of Thoughts and Emotions:** Secular mindfulness practices train individuals to observe their thoughts and emotions as mental events that arise and pass, rather than identifying with them as fixed realities. This helps to create a sense of psychological distance from negative or distressing thoughts and feelings, reducing their impact.
- **Cultivating Kindness and Compassion:** While loving-kindness meditations often explore this more explicitly (as discussed in Chapter 7), secular mindfulness interventions often implicitly or explicitly encourage the development of kindness and compassion toward oneself and others as a natural outgrowth of increased awareness and acceptance.

Diverse Applications of Secular Mindfulness in Modern Life:

The evidence-based effectiveness of secular mindfulness has led to its widespread adoption across a diverse range of settings and applications:

- **Healthcare and Mental Health:** As seen with MBSR and MBCT, secular mindfulness interventions are now widely used in healthcare settings to manage chronic pain, reduce stress and anxiety disorders, prevent relapse in depression, and improve overall well-being in individuals facing various physical and mental health challenges. Research continues to explore its efficacy for conditions such as insomnia, eating disorders, and substance abuse.
- **Education:** Mindfulness-based programs are increasingly being implemented in schools and universities to enhance students' attention spans, improve emotional regulation, reduce stress related to academic pressure, and foster greater self-awareness and social-emotional learning. These programs aim to equip young people with valuable life skills for navigating the challenges of adolescence and beyond.
- **The Workplace:** Organisations recognise the benefits of mindfulness training for employees, including reduced stress and burnout, improved focus and productivity, enhanced creativity and decision-making, and better interpersonal relationships. Mindfulness programs are being offered in various corporate settings to promote

employee well-being and organisational effectiveness.
- **Sports and Performance:** Athletes and performers are increasingly utilising mindfulness techniques to enhance focus, improve concentration under pressure, manage anxiety, and cultivate a greater sense of presence in their performance. Mindfulness can help individuals to access a state of "flow" and perform at their peak.
- **Law and Criminal Justice:** Mindfulness-based interventions are being explored and implemented in the legal profession to reduce stress and burnout among lawyers and judges, and within the criminal justice system to promote rehabilitation, reduce recidivism, and foster empathy and self-awareness among incarcerated individuals.
- **Parenting:** Mindfulness practices are being taught to parents to help them manage the stresses of parenting, cultivate greater patience and empathy, and foster more mindful and attuned relationships with their children.
- **Personal Development and Well-being:** Beyond specific clinical or professional applications, secular mindfulness practices are widely embraced by individuals seeking to enhance their overall well-being, cultivate greater self-awareness, reduce daily stress, and live more fully in the present moment.

The Scientific Basis of Secular Mindfulness:

The widespread adoption of secular mindfulness is largely due to the growing body of scientific evidence supporting its efficacy. Research utilising various methodologies, including neuroimaging studies, physiological measures, and clinical trials, has demonstrated that regular mindfulness practice can lead to significant positive changes in the brain and body, including:

- **Increased Grey Matter Density:** Studies have shown that mindfulness meditation can increase the density of grey matter in brain regions associated with learning, memory, emotional regulation, and self-awareness, such as the hippocampus and the prefrontal cortex.
- **Reduced Amygdala Activity:** The amygdala is the brain region primarily involved in processing fear and stress responses. Research suggests that mindfulness practice can reduce amygdala activity, resulting in decreased feelings of anxiety and reactivity.
- **Enhanced Connectivity:** Mindfulness meditation has been linked to increased connectivity between different brain regions, particularly between the prefrontal cortex (involved in executive functions and emotional regulation) and other areas, suggesting improved self-control and emotional stability.
- **Physiological Benefits:** Studies have shown that mindfulness practice can lead to physiological benefits such as reduced levels of stress hormones (like cortisol), lower blood pressure, improved

immune function, and increased heart rate variability (an indicator of greater resilience to stress).

- **Improved Attention and Focus:** Secular mindfulness training has consistently enhanced attentional control, improved sustained attention, and reduced mind-wandering.

Distinguishing Secular Mindfulness from Its Traditional Roots:

While secular mindfulness draws its core techniques and principles from Buddhist meditation, it is important to acknowledge some key distinctions:

- **Decontextualization:** Secular mindfulness typically removes the religious and philosophical frameworks that traditionally underpin these practices, focusing instead on their psychological and physiological benefits. Concepts such as karma, rebirth, and enlightenment are generally not emphasised.
- **Emphasis on Scientific Validation:** Secular mindfulness strongly emphasises empirical research and scientific evidence to support its efficacy and mechanisms of action.
- **Broad Accessibility:** Secular mindfulness aims to be accessible to individuals of all backgrounds and belief systems, making it more readily integrated into mainstream healthcare, education, and workplace settings.
- **Specific Outcome-Oriented Applications:** Secular mindfulness interventions are often tailored

to address specific outcomes, such as stress reduction, pain management, or relapse prevention, with clearly defined protocols and goals.

Potential Challenges and Considerations for the Future of Secular Mindfulness:

Despite its widespread popularity and demonstrated benefits, the secularisation of mindfulness also presents certain challenges and considerations for the future:

- **Potential for "McMindfulness":** Concerns about the potential for a superficial or overly commodified understanding and application of mindfulness, losing some of its depth and transformative potential in pursuing quick fixes or enhanced productivity.
- **Ethical Considerations:** As mindfulness becomes more integrated into various institutions, ethical considerations regarding privacy, data collection, and the potential for misuse must be carefully addressed.
- **Maintaining the Integrity of the Practice:** Ensuring that the core principles of nonjudgmental awareness and compassion are not diluted or distorted in secularisation is crucial for maintaining the true benefits of mindfulness.
- **The Role of Teachers and Practitioners:** The quality of mindfulness teachers and practitioners remains paramount in ensuring effective and ethical delivery of these interventions. Continued training and professional development are essential.

- **Further Research:** While a significant body of research exists, ongoing and rigorous scientific inquiry is needed to understand further the nuances of mindfulness practice, its long-term effects, and its optimal application for diverse populations and conditions.

In conclusion, the rise of secular mindfulness represents a significant and impactful development in the history of contemplative practices. By bridging the ancient wisdom of Eastern traditions with the rigour of modern science, secular mindfulness has made these powerful tools for cultivating well-being and reducing suffering accessible to a much wider audience. Its continued integration into various aspects of modern life holds immense promise for fostering greater awareness, resilience, and compassion in an increasingly complex and demanding world. However, it is crucial to navigate the challenges and considerations associated with its secularisation thoughtfully, ensuring that the integrity and transformative potential of mindfulness are preserved for future generations.

Meditation Journey

Chapter 6: Cultivating Mindfulness in Daily Life: Weaving Awareness into the Fabric of Existence

While dedicated periods of formal meditation practice, whether seated, walking, or lying down, provide a crucial foundation for cultivating mindfulness, the true transformative power of this practice lies in its ability to extend beyond the cushion and permeate the very fabric of our daily lives. Mindfulness is not merely a technique employed during designated meditation sessions; it is a way of being, a quality of awareness that can be cultivated and integrated into every moment, transforming mundane activities and challenging interactions into opportunities for deeper presence, insight, and connection. This chapter will delve into the practical art of weaving mindfulness into the tapestry of our daily routines, exploring specific strategies and techniques for bringing conscious awareness to a wide range of activities, from the seemingly automatic to the more complex and emotionally charged. By learning to cultivate this continuous thread of mindful awareness, we can move beyond living on autopilot and begin to experience the richness and fullness of each moment as it unfolds.

The Importance of Extending Mindfulness Beyond Formal Practice:

The benefits cultivated during formal meditation sessions, such as increased focus, emotional regulation, and a greater sense of calm, can often feel fleeting if confined to the designated practice time. The real work, and the true reward, of mindfulness lies in our ability to carry this awareness into the hustle and bustle of our daily lives. When mindfulness becomes an integral part of navigating our experiences, it can lead to profound and lasting shifts in our perception, reactions, and overall sense of well-being. Instead of being swept away by the constant stream of thoughts and emotions that often drive our automatic responses, we can begin to approach our experiences with greater intention, clarity, and equanimity. This allows us to respond more skilfully to challenges, appreciate the subtle joys of everyday life, and cultivate a deeper sense of connection with ourselves and the world around us.

Strategies for Integrating Mindfulness into Daily Activities:

The key to cultivating mindfulness in daily life is intentionally bringing your attention to the present moment during routine activities that we often perform on autopilot. Here are some practical strategies for doing so:

- **Mindful Breathing Throughout the Day:** You don't need to sit down for a formal meditation to connect with your breath. Take short pauses throughout the day – while waiting in line, sitting at your desk, or before starting a new task – to bring your awareness to a few cycles of your breath. Notice the sensation of the inhale and the exhale without trying to change it. Even a few mindful breaths can help anchor you in the present moment and interrupt patterns of mind-wandering or stress.

- **Mindful Walking:** Extend the principles of walking meditation (as discussed in Chapter 2) to your everyday walking. Pay attention to the sensations in your feet as they make contact with the ground, the shifting of your weight, the movement of your legs, and the rhythm of your steps. Notice the sights, sounds, and smells around you without getting lost in thought.
- **Mindful Eating:** Transform mealtimes into opportunities for mindful awareness (as briefly introduced in Chapter 3). Before you begin eating, take a moment to appreciate your food's sight, smell, and texture. As you eat, pay attention to the taste, the act of chewing, and the sensations in your mouth and body. Eat slowly and deliberately, noticing when you feel full. Avoid distractions like screens or reading during meals.
- **Mindful Listening:** When engaging in conversations, practice mindful listening. Bring your full attention to the person speaking, noticing their words, tone of voice, and body language. Resist the urge to interrupt or plan your response while they are still talking. Simply be present and listen with genuine curiosity and openness.
- **Mindful Communication:** Extend mindfulness to your own speaking. Before you speak, pause briefly to become aware of your

intention and the words you will use. Speak clearly and with intention, paying attention to your tone of voice and how your words might be received.

- **Mindful Use of Technology:** In our digitally saturated world, technology can often pull us away from the present moment. Practice mindful engagement with your devices. When checking your phone or computer, do so with intention and awareness. Notice how you feel before, during, and after using technology. Set boundaries and create "tech-free" zones or times to cultivate greater presence.
- **Mindful Chores:** Even mundane tasks like washing dishes, doing laundry, or tidying up can become opportunities for mindfulness. Bring your full attention to the physical sensations involved in the activity – the feel of the water on your hands, the scent of the soap, the movement of your body. Notice the details of the task without rushing or thinking about other things.
- **Mindful Transitions:** Consider the transitions between activities throughout your day. As you move from one task to another, briefly pause to notice the shift in your focus and energy. This can help to create a sense of continuity and prevent feeling rushed or scattered.
- **Mindful Sensory Awareness:** Intentionally engage your senses throughout the day. Take a moment to really look at the colours and shapes around you, listen to the sounds of your environment, notice the smells in the air, and feel the textures of things you touch. This can bring a

sense of aliveness and appreciation to the ordinary moments of your day.

Cultivating Mindfulness in Challenging Situations:

Mindfulness is not just about appreciating pleasant moments but also a powerful tool for navigating difficult emotions and challenging interactions with greater skill and equanimity.

- **Mindfulness of Emotions:** When a difficult emotion arises (such as anger, sadness, or anxiety), instead of immediately reacting or trying to suppress it, practice mindful awareness. Notice the physical sensations associated with the emotion in your body (e.g., tightness in the chest, clenching of the jaw). Acknowledge the emotion without judgment ("This is anger"). Observe how the feeling arises, intensifies, and eventually passes. This can help to create space between the emotion and your reaction, allowing for a more skilful response.
- **Mindfulness of Thoughts:** When negative or unhelpful thoughts arise, practice observing them as mental events rather than identifying with them as truths. Notice the content of the thought without getting carried away by its narrative. Recognise that thoughts are just thoughts, not necessarily facts. This can help to lessen their power and emotional impact.
- **Mindful Communication in Conflict:** During disagreements or challenging conversations, maintain mindful awareness of your own emotions and reactions, as well as the emotions and

perspectives of the other person. Practice mindful listening (as described earlier) and respond with intention and clarity rather than automatic reactivity.

- **Mindfulness of Pain and Discomfort:** Consider the sensations when experiencing physical pain or discomfort. Notice the pain's location, intensity, and quality without judgment or resistance. Observe any changes in the sensations over time. This can help to lessen the emotional suffering associated with pain.

Common Obstacles to Daily Mindfulness and How to Overcome Them:

Integrating mindfulness into daily life is not always easy. We often encounter obstacles such as:

- **Busyness and Lack of Time:** Feeling constantly rushed can make it seem impossible to slow down and be mindful. Start small by incorporating brief moments of mindfulness into your existing routines. Even 30 seconds of mindful breathing can make a difference. Gradually increase the duration and frequency as you become more comfortable.
- **Forgetfulness:** It's easy to forget to be mindful during an activity. Use reminders, such as setting an alarm on your phone or placing a visual cue in a prominent place, to prompt you to pause and bring your attention to the present moment.
- **Resistance and Boredom:** Sometimes, bringing awareness to mundane tasks can feel boring or irritating. Approach these moments with

curiosity and a sense of exploration. Notice the subtle details you might usually miss. Remember that even seemingly ordinary moments are part of your life.

- **Self-Judgment:** We may judge ourselves for not being "mindful enough" or for getting distracted. Practice self-compassion and remember that mindfulness is a practice, not a perfect state. Gently redirect your attention when you notice your mind wandering, without criticism.
- **Emotional Overwhelm:** When strong emotions arise, it can be challenging to stay present with them. Start by practising mindfulness during calmer moments, gradually building your capacity to stay present with more intense emotions. If you feel overwhelmed, stepping away and returning to mindfulness is okay when you feel more grounded.

The Long-Term Benefits of a Mindful Life:

Cultivating mindfulness in daily life is not just about managing stress or improving focus in the short term. Over time, it can lead to profound and lasting benefits, including:

- **Increased Joy and Appreciation:** By being more present, we become more attuned to the subtle joys and beauty that often go unnoticed in the rush of daily life.
- **Deeper Connection:** Mindfulness fosters a greater connection with ourselves, others, and the world around us.
- **Greater Resilience:** By observing our thoughts and emotions without reactivity, we

develop greater emotional resilience and the ability to navigate challenges with more skill and composure.

- **Improved Self-Understanding:** Bringing mindful awareness to our inner experiences leads to a deeper understanding of our patterns, triggers, and values.
- **A More Meaningful Life:** Living with greater presence and intention makes us more likely to align our actions with our values and experience a greater sense of purpose and meaning.

Weaving mindfulness into the fabric of our daily existence is a continuous journey, a lifelong practice of waking up to the richness and fullness of each moment. It requires patience, persistence, and a willingness to bring conscious awareness to the ordinary and the extraordinary alike. By intentionally cultivating this quality of presence, we can transform our lives from a series of automatic reactions into a conscious and meaningful unfolding. The potential for deeper connection, greater joy, and increased wisdom lies in our formal meditation sessions and our ability to be fully present in every breath, step, and interaction of our day.

Chapter 7: The Heart Practices: Cultivating Loving-Kindness and Compassion Through Meditation

While mindfulness and concentration practices focus primarily on developing awareness and mental stability, another profound and transformative branch of meditation centres on cultivating positive emotional states, particularly loving-kindness (*mettā*) and compassion (*karuṇā*). These "heart practices," deeply rooted in Buddhist teachings and increasingly embraced in secular contexts, involve intentionally directing feelings of warmth, goodwill, kindness, and empathy towards oneself, loved ones, neutral individuals, difficult people, and ultimately, all beings. Cultivating these qualities through systematic meditation enriches our inner lives, fostering a greater sense of connection and well-being, and can positively transform our relationships and interactions with the world around us. This chapter will delve into the principles and practices of loving-kindness and compassion meditation, exploring their distinct nuances, outlining step-by-step instructions for engaging in these powerful cultivations, and examining their profound benefits for individual and collective well-being.

Meditation Journey

Understanding Loving-Kindness (Mettā): The Foundation of Goodwill

Loving-kindness, often translated from the Pali word *mettā*, encompasses a broad spectrum of positive emotions, including goodwill, benevolence, warmth, friendliness, and a sincere wish for the happiness and well-being of others. It is not merely a sentimental feeling but a cultivated attitude of cherishing and wanting the best for all beings, without discrimination or prejudice. Loving-kindness forms a foundational element of many Buddhist spiritual paths, serving as an antidote to ill-will, aversion, and hatred, and fostering a sense of interconnectedness and universal fraternity.

Key Principles of Loving-Kindness:

- **Universal Scope:** While it often begins with oneself and loved ones, the intention of loving-kindness gradually expands to encompass all beings, including those we find challenging or neutral.
- **Wish for Well-being:** The core of loving-kindness is the sincere and heartfelt wish for others to be free from suffering and to experience happiness, peace, and joy.
- **Absence of Attachment:** Loving-kindness is not rooted in attachment or expectation of reciprocation. It is a selfless offering of goodwill.
- **Antidote to Negativity:** Cultivating loving-kindness is a powerful counterforce to negative emotions such as anger, resentment, and fear,

promoting a more positive and compassionate inner state.

Step-by-Step Instructions for Loving-Kindness Meditation:

1. **Preparation:** Find a quiet, comfortable space to sit or lie undisturbed. Take a few deep breaths to settle your body and mind.

2. **Focus on Yourself:** Begin by directing feelings of loving-kindness towards yourself. This is a crucial step, as it can be difficult to genuinely extend kindness to others if we do not cultivate it within ourselves. Silently repeat phrases such as:

    - "May I be filled with loving-kindness."
    - "May I be well."
    - "May I be peaceful and at ease."
    - "May I be happy." Feel the sincerity of these wishes in your heart. Visualize yourself surrounded by a warm and gentle light.

3. **Extend to a Loved One:** Once you feel a sense of loving-kindness towards yourself, gently extend these feelings towards someone you deeply care about – a family member, a close friend, or a beloved pet. Visualize their face and repeat the phrases, directing them specifically:

    - "May you be filled with loving-kindness."
    - "May you be well."

Meditation Journey
- "May you be peaceful and at ease."
- "May you be happy." Feel the warmth of your care and affection flowing towards them.

4. **Extend to a Neutral Person:** Next, bring to mind someone towards whom you feel neutral – perhaps a neighbour you see occasionally, a cashier at your local store, or someone you pass on your commute. Visualize their face and repeat the loving-kindness phrases, directing your goodwill towards them without any particular attachment or strong emotion:

- "May you be filled with loving-kindness."
- "May you be well."
- "May you be peaceful and at ease."
- "May you be happy." Practice extending your wish for their well-being simply because they are a fellow human being.

5. **Extend to a Difficult Person:** This step can be challenging, but it is a powerful aspect of cultivating universal loving-kindness. Bring to mind someone with whom you have had difficulties or towards whom you harbour negative feelings. Begin by acknowledging your feelings without judgment. Then, gently and with as much sincerity as you can muster, direct the loving-kindness phrases towards them:

- "May you be filled with loving-kindness."
- "May you be well."
- "May you be peaceful and at ease."
- "May you be happy."

You may find it helpful to start with a less difficult person and gradually work your way towards those who evoke stronger negative emotions. The aim here is not necessarily to suddenly feel strong affection, but rather to cultivate a wish for their suffering to end.

6. **Extend to All Beings:** Finally, expand your circle of loving-kindness to encompass all beings – all people, all animals, all creatures, without exception. Visualize the entire world and repeat the phrases, allowing your goodwill to radiate outwards:

- "May all beings be filled with loving-kindness."
- "May all beings be well."
- "May all beings be peaceful and at ease."
- "May all beings be happy."

Feel a sense of interconnectedness and universal compassion flowing from your heart.

7. **Sustaining the Practice:** Continue this meditation for a comfortable period, perhaps 10-20 minutes. You can return to any of the stages as needed. Pay attention to the feelings that arise in your heart as you direct these wishes.

Understanding Compassion (Karuṇā): The Wish to Alleviate Suffering

Compassion, often translated from the Pali word *karuṇā*, is closely related to loving-kindness but focuses specifically on alleviating suffering. It is the heartfelt recognition of oneself and others' pain and distress, coupled with a sincere desire to alleviate that suffering. Compassion arises from understanding our shared human vulnerability and the interconnectedness of all beings who experience pain and hardship.

Key Principles of Compassion:

- **Recognition of Suffering:** Compassion begins with a clear and empathetic recognition of suffering in oneself and others.
- **Heartfelt Concern:** It involves a genuine feeling of concern and sorrow for those who are experiencing pain.
- **Active Wish to Help:** Compassion is not passive pity; it is accompanied by a strong desire to alleviate suffering and its causes.
- **Universality:** Like loving-kindness, compassion extends to all beings without discrimination.

Step-by-Step Instructions for Compassion Meditation:

1. **Preparation:** Find a quiet and comfortable space. Take a few deep breaths to settle.

2. **Focus on Your Own Suffering:** Consider a time when you experienced suffering – perhaps physical pain, emotional distress, or a difficult situation. Gently acknowledge this suffering without judgment. Repeat phrases to yourself, such as:

- "May I be free from this suffering."
- "May I find relief from this pain."
- "May I have the strength to bear this."

Feel empathy and understanding for your own experience.

3. **Extend to the Suffering of a Loved One:** Bring to mind someone you care about who is currently experiencing suffering. Visualize their situation and repeat phrases with the sincere wish for their pain to be eased:

- "May you be free from this suffering."
- "May you find relief from this pain."
- "May you have the strength to bear this." Feel your heart open to their pain and your desire for their well-being.

4. **Extend to the Suffering of a Neutral Person:** Bring to mind someone towards whom you feel neutral who you know is likely experiencing some form of suffering (e.g., someone who is ill, someone facing hardship). Repeat the phrases, extending your wish for their suffering to be alleviated:

- "May you be free from this suffering."
- "May you find relief from this pain."

- "May you have the strength to bear this."

5. **Extend to the Suffering of a Difficult Person:** Bring to mind someone with whom you have had difficulties or who has caused you pain, and consider the suffering they may be experiencing, whether obvious or hidden. Gently repeat the phrases, wishing for their suffering to end:

    - "May you be free from this suffering."
    - "May you find relief from this pain."
    - "May you have the strength to bear this." This step can be challenging, but it helps to break down barriers and cultivate a more universal sense of empathy.

6. **Extend to the Suffering of All Beings:** Expand your awareness to encompass all beings experiencing suffering – those who are sick, hungry, afraid, grieving, or in any form of pain. Repeat the phrases, allowing your compassion to radiate outwards:

    - "May all beings be free from suffering."
    - "May all beings find relief from their pain."
    - "May all beings have the strength to bear their difficulties."

7. **Sustaining the Practice:** Continue this meditation for a comfortable duration, allowing the

feelings of empathy and the wish to alleviate suffering to resonate within you.

The Interconnectedness of Loving-Kindness and Compassion:

While loving-kindness focuses on the wish for happiness and well-being, and compassion focuses on the wish to alleviate suffering, these two heart practices are deeply interconnected and mutually reinforcing. Loving-kindness provides the warm and benevolent foundation upon which compassion can arise. When we genuinely wish for others to be happy, we are naturally more inclined to feel concern and empathy when we recognise their suffering and to desire its end. Cultivating loving-kindness and compassion creates a more balanced and complete cultivation of a caring and open heart.

Benefits of Loving-Kindness and Compassion Meditation:

The consistent practice of loving-kindness and compassion meditation can yield a wide range of profound benefits:

- **Increased Positive Emotions:** These practices cultivate feelings of warmth, joy, gratitude, and interconnectedness, leading to a more positive emotional baseline.
- **Reduced Negative Emotions:** These practices actively cultivate positive emotions, which serve as a powerful antidote to anger, hatred, fear, and anxiety.

- **Improved Relationships:** Cultivating loving-kindness and compassion can enhance our empathy, understanding, and patience in our interactions with others, leading to more harmonious and fulfilling relationships.
- **Increased Self-Compassion:** Directing lovingkindness and compassion toward ourselves helps cultivate greater self-acceptance, reduce self-criticism, and foster a stronger sense of inner peace.
- **Reduced Stress and Anxiety:** These practices can help calm the nervous system and reduce overall stress and anxiety by promoting feelings of warmth and connection.
- **Greater Sense of Purpose and Meaning:** Connecting with a sense of universal care and compassion can imbue life with a deeper sense of purpose and meaning.
- **Improved Physical Health:** Some studies suggest that cultivating positive emotions like loving-kindness and compassion can positively affect physical health, such as lowering blood pressure and improving immune function.

Challenges in Cultivating Loving-Kindness and Compassion:

While the benefits are significant, cultivating loving-kindness and compassion can also present challenges:

- **Difficulty with Self-Compassion:** Many people find it easier to extend kindness to others than to themselves. It is important to be patient and persistent in directing loving-kindness inwards.

- **Resistance Towards Difficult People:** It can be challenging to genuinely wish well for those who have harmed us or caused us pain. Start slowly and focus on the wish for their suffering to end, rather than forcing feelings of affection.
- **Emotional Blockages:** Past traumas or deep-seated negative emotions can sometimes make accessing feelings of warmth and compassion difficult. Gentle and consistent practice can help gradually soften these blockages.
- **Feeling Insincere:** The phrases may sometimes feel like words without genuine emotion. Continue practising with intention, and the feelings will often deepen over time.

Integrating Loving-Kindness and Compassion into Daily Life:

As with mindfulness, the benefits of loving-kindness and compassion are amplified when we extend these qualities beyond our formal meditation practice and weave them into our daily interactions. This can involve:

- **Setting an Intention:** Start your day with the intention of being kind and compassionate toward yourself and others.
- **Brief Reflections:** Taking short moments throughout the day to send silent wishes of loving-kindness or compassion to people you encounter.
- **Mindful Communication:** Speaking with kindness and empathy, even in challenging conversations.

Meditation Journey

- **Acts of Service:** Engaging in small acts of kindness and generosity.
- **Cultivating Empathy:** Actively trying to understand the perspectives and suffering of others.

Cultivating loving-kindness and compassion through meditation is a profound journey of opening the heart and fostering a deeper connection with ourselves and all beings. By intentionally nurturing these qualities, we enhance our well-being and contribute to a more caring and compassionate world. These heart practices offer a powerful antidote to the negativity and division that can often dominate our inner and outer landscapes, guiding us towards a more connected, peaceful, and humane existence.

Sources and related content

www.goodgriefdoula.com

community.beliefnet.com

Chapter 8: Finding Stillness in Motion: The Practice of Movement-Based Meditation

While the image of meditation often conjures stillness – a seated figure in quiet contemplation – the path to inner peace and heightened awareness is not exclusively found in immobility. For many, the body's natural inclination towards movement can become a powerful and accessible avenue for cultivating mindfulness and presence. Movement-based meditation encompasses diverse practices that intentionally integrate physical movement with focused awareness, allowing us to tap into a more profound sense of embodiment and experience the flow of our inner and outer landscapes in a more direct and integrated way. This chapter will explore various forms of movement-based meditation, delving into their historical origins, outlining their core principles and techniques, and providing more comprehensive guidance for engaging in these dynamic and grounding practices.

The Innate Connection Between Movement and Awareness:

From the earliest forms of human expression through dance and ritual to the intuitive way we often pace when deep in thought, movement has always been intrinsically linked to our inner states. Movement can be a powerful catalyst for releasing tension, regulating emotions, and focusing attention. When consciously combined with mindful awareness, it transcends mere physical exercise. It becomes a profound form of meditation, allowing us to connect with the present moment through the sensations of our bodies in motion. For individuals who find sustained stillness challenging due to physical discomfort, restlessness, or a naturally more kinetic disposition, movement-based meditation can offer a more accessible and engaging entry into the benefits of contemplative practice.

Key Principles of Movement-Based Meditation:

While the specific techniques vary widely, most forms of movement-based meditation share several core principles:

- **Mindful Attention to Bodily Sensations:** The primary focus is on bringing conscious awareness to the physical sensations that arise during movement – the feeling of muscles stretching, the shifting of weight, the rhythm of steps, the flow of energy.
- **Synchronisation of Movement and Awareness:** The intention is to consciously link physical movements with mental focus, creating a unified body-mind experience in the present moment.
- **Gentle and Deliberate Action:** The movements involved are often performed slowly and deliberately, allowing for a heightened awareness of each subtle shift and sensation. However, some

forms can incorporate more dynamic yet still mindful movement.

- **Non-Judgmental Observation:** As with seated meditation, one should be nonjudgmental about thoughts, feelings, and sensations that arise during movement, allowing them to come and go without getting carried away.
- **Cultivating Presence Through Embodiment:** Movement-based meditation encourages a more profound sense of embodiment, fully embracing our physical experience and anchoring us in the here and now.

Exploring Different Forms of Movement-Based Meditation:

The spectrum of movement-based meditation practices is broad and encompasses traditions from various cultures and spiritual lineages:

- **Walking Meditation (Vipassanā Walking):** Rooted in Buddhist Vipassanā practice (briefly introduced in Chapter 2 and expanded in Chapter 6), walking meditation involves bringing mindful awareness to the sensations of walking. It can be practised slowly and deliberately, focusing on lifting, moving forward, and placing each foot down. Variations include noting the intention to move, the initiation, actual movement, and placement. It can be practised indoors or outdoors, providing an accessible way to cultivate mindfulness in motion.

Step-by-Step Instructions for Walking Meditation:

1. **Find a Space:** Choose a safe and relatively quiet space where you can walk a short distance back and forth.
2. **Posture:** Stand with your feet hip-width apart, your arms relaxed at your sides or clasped gently in front of you. Maintain a relaxed but upright posture.
3. **Grounding:** Take a few moments to feel the soles of your feet making contact with the ground. Notice the pressure and any sensations of warmth or coolness.
4. **Initiating Movement:** Begin to walk slowly and deliberately. Bring your awareness to the intention to lift your foot, the feeling of lifting it, the movement forward through space, the feeling of placing your foot down, and the shifting of your weight.
5. **Focus on Sensations:** Pay close attention to the physical sensations in your feet, legs, and body as you walk. Notice the subtle shifts in balance, the movement of your muscles, and the rhythm of your steps.
6. **Synchronisation with Breath (Optional):** You can coordinate your breath with your steps, perhaps taking one or two steps on the inhale and one or two on the exhale.
7. **Dealing with Distractions:** When your mind wanders (as it will), gently acknowledge the distraction without

judgment and bring your attention back to the sensations of walking.

8. **Turning:** When you reach the end of your walking path, pause briefly, become aware of the intention to turn, and then turn slowly and mindfully, paying attention to the sensations of movement as you change direction.

9. **Duration:** Practice comfortably, starting with 10-15 minutes and gradually increasing as desired.

- **Mindful Movement in Yoga (Hatha Yoga):** While the physical postures (*asanas*) of Hatha Yoga are often emphasised for their physical benefits, when practised with conscious awareness of the breath and bodily sensations, they become a powerful form of movement-based meditation. Holding poses with mindful attention allows for a deeper exploration of physical and mental stillness within movement. At the same time, the following sequences (vinyasas) can cultivate a continuous awareness of the body in motion.

Key Aspects of Mindful Yoga Practice:

- **Breath Synchronisation:** Consciously linking each movement with the inhale and exhale, creating a flowing rhythm of breath and motion.
- **Body Awareness:** Pay close attention to stretching, contracting, and balancing sensations in each pose.

Meditation Journey

- **Present Moment Focus:** Bringing your awareness fully to the current pose and the sensations arising, letting go of thoughts about the past or future.
- **Non-Striving:** Approaching the practice with a sense of gentle exploration rather than forceful exertion or competition.
- **Mindful Transitions:** Paying attention to the movements between poses, maintaining a continuous thread of awareness.

- **Tai Chi and Qigong:** These ancient Chinese movement systems, often described as "meditation in motion," involve slow, flowing, and deliberate movements coordinated with breath. Tai Chi emphasises balance, coordination, and the circulation of Qi (vital energy). At the same time, Qigong encompasses a wider range of movements and postures to cultivate and harmonise *Qi* for health, well-being, and spiritual development. Through gentle, rhythmic movement, both practices cultivate a deep sense of body awareness, presence, and inner stillness.

Core Principles of Tai Chi and Qigong:

- **Slow and Deliberate Movement:** Performing movements with conscious control and attention to detail.
- **Breath Coordination:** Synchronising movements with the natural rhythm of the breath.

- **Focus on *Qi* (Energy):** Cultivating awareness and the smooth flow of vital energy throughout the body.
- **Balance and Grounding:** Developing physical and mental stability through mindful movement.
- **Integration of Mind and Body:** Fostering a unified experience of physical action and inner awareness.

• **Mindful Dance:** This practice involves moving freely and intuitively while maintaining conscious awareness of bodily sensations, emotions, and the present moment. It can be a powerful way to release tension, explore self-expression, and connect with the body's innate wisdom. There are various forms of mindful dance, often emphasising non-judgmental exploration and authentic movement.

Key Aspects of Mindful Dance:

- **Freedom of Movement:** Allowing the body to move spontaneously without prescribed steps or choreography.
- **Sensory Awareness:** Paying attention to the physical sensations of movement, such as weight, momentum, and contact with the ground.
- **Emotional Expression:** Allowing emotions to arise and be expressed through movement without judgment.

Meditation Journey

- **Present Moment Focus:** Staying present with the unfolding experience of movement and sensation.
- **Non-Goal Orientation:** Focusing on the process of moving rather than achieving a specific outcome or aesthetic.

- **Other Rhythmic and Repetitive Movements:** Various other activities can be transformed into forms of movement-based meditation by bringing conscious awareness to the physical sensations involved. These can include:

  - **Mindful Gardening:** Paying attention to the feel of the soil, the movement of your hands, the scents of the plants.
  - **Mindful Sweeping or Cleaning:** Focusing on the physical actions of the task, the movement of your body, the textures and sounds involved.
  - **Mindful Knitting or Crafting:** Bringing awareness to your hands' repetitive motions, the materials' textures, and the unfolding creation.

Benefits of Movement-Based Meditation:

Engaging in movement-based meditation practices offers a wide range of benefits that complement those of seated meditation:

- **Increased Body Awareness:** These practices foster a deeper connection with and understanding of the physical body and its sensations.
- **Release of Physical Tension:** Mindful movement can help to release chronic muscle tension and improve flexibility and range of motion.
- **Improved Balance and Coordination:** Tai Chi and mindful walking can enhance physical stability and coordination.
- **Emotional Regulation:** Movement can be a powerful way to process and release emotions healthily and embodied.
- **Enhanced Presence and Focus:** These practices cultivate a strong sense of presence in the here and now by linking movement with awareness.
- **Greater Accessibility:** For those who find stillness challenging, movement-based meditation offers a more engaging and sustainable path to mindfulness.
- **Integration of Mind and Body:** These practices help to bridge the often-perceived gap between the mental and physical aspects of our experience, fostering a more holistic sense of self.
- **Stress Reduction:** The combination of mindful attention and gentle movement can effectively reduce stress and promote relaxation.

Challenges and Considerations in Movement-Based Meditation:

While offering many benefits, movement-based meditation can also present certain challenges:

- **Maintaining Focus Amidst Movement:** It can sometimes be more challenging to maintain sustained attention when the body is in motion than when it is still. Consistent practice and gentle redirection of focus are key.
- **Distraction by the Environment:** External stimuli can be more distracting when practising outdoors or in busy environments. Choosing appropriate spaces and cultivating strong internal awareness can help.
- **Physical Limitations:** Individuals with physical limitations may need to adapt practices or choose forms of movement that are accessible and comfortable for their bodies.
- **The "Exercise" Mindset:** It's important to approach movement-based meditation with mindful exploration rather than striving for physical exertion or achievement.
- **Patience and Consistency:** As with any form of meditation, it takes time and consistent practice to cultivate deeper levels of awareness and experience the full benefits.

Integrating Movement-Based Meditation into Your Life:

Incorporating movement-based meditation into your routine can be an enjoyable and straightforward way to enhance your mindfulness practice:

- **Start Small:** Begin with short sessions of mindful walking or a few minutes of mindful stretching.

- **Choose Activities You Enjoy:** Select forms of movement that resonate with your interests and physical capabilities.
- **Be Patient and Kind to Yourself:** There will be times when your mind wanders. Gently bring your attention back to the sensations of movement.
- **Experiment:** Explore different forms of movement-based meditation to find what works best for you.
- **Integrate into Daily Activities:** Bring mindful awareness to everyday movements like walking to your car or doing household chores.

Finding stillness in motion is a powerful reminder that mindfulness is not limited to a particular posture or environment. By consciously engaging our bodies in movement, we can tap into a deeper level of presence and experience the interconnectedness of our inner and outer worlds in a dynamic and embodied way. Movement-based meditation offers a vibrant and accessible path to cultivating awareness, reducing stress, and finding a sense of flow and harmony amid our active lives.

Meditation Journey

Chapter 9: The Guiding Voice and the Inner Eye: Exploring Guided Meditations and Visualisations

In the vast landscape of meditation practices, guided meditations and visualisations offer particularly accessible and often deeply engaging pathways to cultivating mindfulness, relaxation, and inner transformation. Unlike silent forms of meditation that rely solely on one's own internal focus, guided practices utilise the power of spoken instruction and evocative imagery to direct attention, facilitate relaxation, and promote specific mental and emotional states. This chapter will delve into the nature and benefits of guided meditations and visualisations, explore various types and techniques, and provide more comprehensive guidance on effectively engaging with these powerful tools for inner exploration and growth.

The Nature and Benefits of Guided Meditation:

Guided meditation involves listening to a recording or live instruction that verbally leads you through a meditation practice. The guide typically provides cues and suggestions on where to focus your attention, what to notice in your body and mind, and sometimes offers specific imagery or affirmations to support the meditation's intention. The benefits of guided meditation are numerous and make it a particularly valuable tool for both beginners and experienced meditators:

- **Accessibility for Beginners:** The guidance provided for those new to meditation can make the practice feel less daunting and easier to follow. The verbal instructions help to anchor attention and reduce the feeling of being "lost" in thought.
- **Reduced Mental Effort:** The guiding voice can help to lessen the mental effort required to direct and sustain attention, allowing for deeper relaxation and a more effortless experience.
- **Exploration of Different Techniques:** Guided meditations can introduce practitioners to mindfulness techniques, visualisation practices, and emotional cultivation exercises they might not otherwise explore.
- **Targeting Specific Goals:** Many guided meditations are designed with specific intentions, such as stress reduction, sleep improvement, pain management, cultivating self-compassion, or exploring spiritual themes. This allows individuals to choose practices that address their current needs and goals directly.
- **Deepening Relaxation:** The soothing tone of the guide's voice and the suggestions for relaxation can often lead to a deeper state of physical and mental calm.
- **Emotional Support:** Guided meditations focused on emotions like loving-kindness or forgiveness can provide a supportive framework for processing and transforming difficult feelings.

- **Enhanced Visualisation:** The verbal cues can help to spark and deepen the ability to create vivid and impactful mental imagery.

Exploring Different Types of Guided Meditations:

The world of guided meditation is rich and diverse, offering a wide array of approaches and focuses:

- **Mindfulness of Breath and Body:** Many guided meditations focus on bringing awareness to the breath and various sensations throughout the body. These practices are similar to unguided mindfulness practices but with verbal cues to direct attention.
- **Body Scan Meditations:** As discussed in Chapter 6, guided body scans systematically lead you through different parts of the body, encouraging you to notice any sensations present without judgment.
- **Loving-Kindness and Compassion Meditations:** Guided practices can be particularly helpful in cultivating feelings of warmth, goodwill, and empathy toward oneself and others. They often use specific phrases and visualizations (as explored in Chapter 7).
- **Stress Reduction and Relaxation Meditations:** These often incorporate progressive muscle relaxation, guided imagery of peaceful scenes, and calming breathwork to promote deep relaxation and reduce stress.

- **Sleep Meditations:** Specifically designed to prepare the mind and body for sleep, these meditations often involve gentle relaxation techniques, soothing imagery, and a calming tone of voice.
- **Pain Management Meditations:** Guided practices can help individuals to shift their relationship with chronic pain by focusing on different aspects of the sensation, cultivating acceptance, and reducing emotional reactivity.
- **Spiritual and Insight-Oriented Meditations:** Some guided meditations explore spiritual themes or philosophical concepts, or encourage introspection and self-inquiry.
- **Visualisation Meditations:** These practices heavily rely on the power of mental imagery to create specific experiences or promote desired outcomes, which we will explore in more detail in the next section.

The Power and Potential of Visualisation Meditation:

Visualisation meditation involves using your imagination to create vivid mental images, scenarios, or sensory experiences. These mental constructs can be used for various purposes: relaxation, healing, goal setting, emotional processing, and spiritual exploration. The power of visualization lies in the mind-body connection – our brains often respond to vivid mental imagery as if it were a real experience, triggering corresponding physiological and emotional responses.

Key Principles of Effective Visualisation:

- **Clarity and Detail:** The more vivid and detailed your visualisations, the more impactful they tend to be. Engage as many of your senses as possible – sight, sound, smell, taste, touch, and even kinaesthetic sensations (the feeling of movement).
- **Emotional Engagement:** Infuse your visualisations with positive emotions about your intention. Feel the joy of achieving your goal, the peace of a relaxed state, or the warmth of self-compassion.
- **Regular Practice:** Like any form of meditation, consistent practice enhances the effectiveness of visualisation. Regular engagement strengthens your ability to create and sustain vivid imagery.
- **Belief and Intention:** Approaching your visualisations with a sense of belief in their potential can significantly enhance their impact. Clearly define your intention for the visualisation.
- **Present Moment Focus:** While visualising a future outcome or a different scene, maintain a sense of presence in visualising itself.

Types and Techniques of Visualisation Meditation:

Visualisation can be incorporated into various meditation practices, both guided and unguided:

Meditation Journey

- **Relaxation and Stress Reduction:** Visualise yourself in a peaceful and calming environment, such as a serene beach, a tranquil forest, or a cosy cabin. Engage your senses – feel the sun's warmth, hear the gentle sounds of nature, smell the fresh air.
- **Healing and Well-being:** Visualise your body as healthy and vibrant, focusing on areas that need healing. Imagine a warm, healing light flowing through these areas, promoting regeneration and well-being.
- **Goal Setting and Manifestation:** Imagine yourself having already achieved your goals. Experience the feelings of success, joy, and accomplishment. Engage your senses in the imagined scenario.
- **Emotional Processing:** Visualise yourself gently holding and comforting difficult emotions, allowing them to be present without judgment and gradually releasing them. You might imagine these emotions as clouds passing by or energy gently dissipating.
- **Cultivating Positive Qualities:** Visualise yourself embodying qualities you wish to develop, such as confidence, courage, or compassion. Imagine feeling these qualities radiating from within you and influencing your interactions with people and the world.
- **Spiritual Exploration:** Visualise yourself connecting with a source of wisdom or spiritual guidance, experiencing a sense of unity or transcendence.
- **Future Pacing:** Imagine yourself navigating future situations with confidence and skill,

rehearsing positive responses and outcomes in your mind.

Integrating Guided Meditations and Visualisations into Your Practice:

Guided meditations and visualisations can be easily incorporated into your meditation routine:

- **Utilise Available Resources:** Numerous apps, websites, and podcasts offer guided meditations on various topics and durations. Experiment to find voices and styles that resonate with you.
- **Follow Your Intuition:** Choose guided meditations that align with your current needs and intentions. If you're feeling stressed, opt for a relaxation-focused practice. If you want to cultivate more self-compassion, choose a loving-kindness guided meditation.
- **Create Your Own Guided Meditations:** Once you become more familiar with the format, you can create your own guided meditations tailored to your specific needs and preferences. You can record your own voice or simply guide yourself mentally.
- **Combine Visualisation with Silent Practice:** You can incorporate visualisation techniques into your silent meditation periods. For example, after settling into stillness, you might spend a few minutes visualising a peaceful scene or focusing on a healing light within your body.

- **Be Open and Experiment:** Don't be afraid to try different guided meditations and visualisation techniques. What resonates with you may change over time.
- **Listen Actively:** When engaging with a guided meditation, follow the instructions and allow the imagery to unfold in your mind.
- **Be Patient:** It may take time to develop the ability to create vivid and sustained visualisations. Be patient with yourself and continue practising.

Potential Challenges and How to Navigate Them:

While generally accessible, engaging with guided meditations and visualisations can sometimes present challenges:

- **Distraction by the Guide's Voice:** Occasionally, the tone or pacing of a guide's voice may be distracting. Experiment with different guides until you find one that is soothing and easy to follow.
- **Difficulty with Visualisation:** Some individuals find it challenging to create vivid mental images. Don't get discouraged. Focus on engaging whatever senses you can and allow the imagery to be as subtle or detailed as possible.
- **Mind Wandering:** As with any meditation, your mind may wander during a guided practice. Gently bring your attention back to the guide's voice or the visualisation.
- **Emotional Reactions:** Guided meditations, particularly those focused on emotions or past

experiences, may sometimes bring up unexpected feelings. Allow these emotions to arise without judgment and observe them with compassion. If they become overwhelming, gently bring your focus back to your breath or a neutral sensation.

- **Falling Asleep:** Relaxation-focused guided meditations can sometimes lead to drowsiness. If this is a frequent issue, try practising in a more upright posture or when you are more alert.

Guided meditations and visualisations offer powerful and versatile tools to deepen our inner exploration and cultivate positive states of mind. Whether you seek relaxation, emotional healing, or a more vivid connection with your inner world, these practices provide accessible and engaging pathways to unlock the transformative potential of your own mind. By embracing the guiding voice and nurturing your inner eye, you can embark on a rich and rewarding journey of self-discovery and well-being.

Meditation Journey

Chapter 10: Meditation as a Tool for Transformation: Addressing Specific Challenges

While the general benefits of meditation, such as stress reduction, improved focus, and enhanced emotional regulation, are widely acknowledged, its transformative potential extends to addressing specific challenges many individuals face. By tailoring mindfulness and other meditative techniques, we can cultivate greater resilience, develop healthier coping mechanisms, and foster profound healing in areas such as anxiety, depression, chronic pain, sleep disturbances, and trauma. This chapter will delve into the application of meditation as a targeted tool for navigating these common challenges, exploring specific practices and approaches that can offer significant support and promote well-being.

Meditation for Anxiety: Cultivating Calm in the Face of Worry

Anxiety, characterised by excessive worry, nervousness, and unease, can significantly impact daily functioning and overall quality of life. Meditation, particularly mindfulness-based practices, offers powerful tools for cultivating a different relationship with anxious thoughts and physical sensations:

- **Mindful Observation of Anxious Thoughts:** Instead of getting caught up in the content of anxious thoughts, mindfulness teaches us to observe them as mental events that arise and pass without judgment or the need to analyse or fix them. By creating this psychological distance, we can lessen their power and emotional grip.
- **Body Awareness and Anxiety:** Anxiety often manifests physically through sensations like a racing heart, shortness of breath, or muscle tension. Body scan meditations and mindful attention to these sensations can help us become more aware of the early signs of anxiety, allowing us to respond more effectively before it escalates.
- **Anchoring in the Present Moment:** Anxiety often revolves around worries about the future. Mindfulness practices, particularly focusing on the breath or bodily sensations, anchor us in the present moment, providing a refuge from future-oriented anxieties.
- **Acceptance and Non-Resistance:** Resisting or trying to suppress anxious feelings can often intensify them. Mindfulness encourages acceptance of these feelings as temporary experiences, allowing them to flow and eventually subside more naturally.

Specific Practices for Anxiety:

- **Breath Awareness Meditation:** Focusing intently on the sensation of the breath entering and leaving the body can serve as a stable anchor during moments of anxiety.

- **Body Scan for Tension Release:** Systematically scanning the body for areas of tension and consciously relaxing them can alleviate the physical manifestations of anxiety.
- **"RAIN" Technique:** This acronym stands for Recognise, Allow, Investigate, Nurture. It's a mindfulness-based approach to working with difficult emotions like anxiety. It involves acknowledging the feeling, allowing it to be present without resistance, investigating the sensations in the body, and nurturing oneself with compassion.

Meditation for Depression: Finding Light in the Darkness

Depression, characterised by persistent sadness, loss of interest, and feelings of hopelessness, can be a debilitating condition. While meditation is not a replacement for conventional treatment, it can be a valuable complementary tool for managing symptoms and fostering a sense of well-being:

- **Mindfulness-Based Cognitive Therapy (MBCT):** As discussed in Chapter 5, MBCT integrates explicitly mindfulness practices with cognitive behavioural therapy to help individuals become aware of and disengage from negative thought patterns that can trigger depressive episodes.
- **Observing Negative Thoughts as Thoughts:** Similar to anxiety, mindfulness helps us to recognise depressive thoughts as mental events rather than

absolute truths. This can reduce identification with these thoughts and lessen their impact.
- **Cultivating Present Moment Awareness:** Depression often involves rumination about the past. Mindfulness anchors us in the present, offering moments of respite from these negative cycles.
- **Body Awareness and Depression:** Depression can manifest physically as fatigue and a lack of energy. Gentle body awareness practices can help reconnect with physical sensations and potentially increase a sense of embodiment.
- **Loving-Kindness and Self-Compassion:** Practices that cultivate warmth, kindness, and understanding towards oneself can be particularly beneficial in counteracting the self-criticism and negativity often associated with depression.

Specific Practices for Depression:

- **Mindfulness of Pleasant Events:** Intentionally focusing on and savouring moments of joy or pleasant experiences can help counteract the tendency towards negativity.
- **Walking Meditation with Awareness of Sensory Input:** Engaging with the environment through mindful walking can gently re-engage with the world and counteract feelings of withdrawal.
- **Self-Compassion Breaks:** Short practices involving acknowledging one's suffering, recognising it as part of the human

experience, and offering oneself kindness and understanding.

Meditation for Chronic Pain: Finding Peace Amidst Discomfort

Chronic pain can be physically and emotionally draining. Meditation offers strategies for shifting our relationship with pain and reducing its overall impact:

- **Mindful Observation of Pain Sensations:** Instead of fighting or resisting pain, mindfulness encourages us to observe its qualities – location, intensity, texture – without judgment. This can help deconstruct the experience of pain and reduce the associated emotional suffering.
- **Acceptance of Pain:** While not about liking pain, acceptance involves acknowledging its presence without constant struggle. This can paradoxically lead to a reduction in the perceived intensity of pain and an increase in coping abilities.
- **Focusing on What is Not Painful:** Mindfulness can help us broaden our awareness beyond pain, noticing other sensations in the body and the surrounding environment. It reminds us that pain is not the entirety of our experience.
- **Reducing Catastrophizing:** Chronic pain can often be accompanied by negative thoughts and fears about the future. Mindfulness helps to observe these thoughts without getting carried away by them.

Specific Practices for Chronic Pain:

- **Body Scan with Gentle Inquiry:** Systematically scanning the body, paying attention to areas of pain with a gentle and curious attitude, noticing any subtle shifts or changes.
- **Breath Awareness Around Pain:** Focusing on the breath as it moves through the body, noticing any connection or lack thereof with the area of pain.
- **Visualisation of Comfort:** Gently visualising a sense of warmth, soothing light, or spaciousness around the area of pain.

Meditation for Sleep Disturbances: Cultivating a Calm Mind for Rest

Sleep disturbances like insomnia can be significantly improved through meditation practices that promote relaxation and quiet the mind:

- **Reducing Pre-Sleep Rumination:** Mindfulness helps disengage from the worrying and planning cycle that often keeps us awake at night.
- **Calming the Nervous System:** Practices like breath awareness and body scans can activate the parasympathetic nervous system, promoting relaxation and preparing the body for sleep.
- **Acceptance of Thoughts:** Learning to observe thoughts without getting involved can prevent the "racing mind" that often accompanies insomnia.

- **Creating a Relaxing Pre-Sleep Routine:** Incorporating gentle meditation practices into a bedtime routine can signal to the body and mind that it's time to wind down.

Specific Practices for Sleep:

- **Breath Awareness with Lengthened Exhalations:** Focusing on slow, deep breaths with a slightly longer exhale can promote relaxation.
- **Body Scan for Relaxation:** A gentle body scan in bed can help release physical tension that might be hindering sleep.
- **Guided Sleep Meditations:** Many guided meditations specifically focus on creating a calm and peaceful state conducive to sleep, often using soothing imagery and a calming voice.

Meditation for Trauma: Gentle Presence and Reconnection

Working with trauma through meditation requires a sensitive and often gradual approach, and it's crucial to do so with the guidance of a trauma-informed therapist. Mindfulness can be a valuable tool for survivors of trauma when practised safely and mindfully:

- **Developing Body Awareness in a Safe Way:** Gentle body awareness practices can help survivors reconnect with their bodies in a safe and

manageable way, gradually reclaiming a sense of embodiment.
- **Observing Sensations Without Judgment:** Learning to observe physical sensations, including those related to traumatic memories, with curiosity and nonjudgment can help reduce fear and reactivity.
- **Grounding Techniques:** Mindfulness of the breath or the body's feeling of contact with the ground can be powerful grounding techniques that can bring one back to the present moment during distress.
- **Cultivating Self-Compassion:** Practices that foster kindness and understanding towards oneself are crucial for healing from trauma.

Specific Practices for Trauma (with professional guidance):

- **Gentle Breath Awareness:** Focusing on the natural rhythm of the breath as a safe anchor.
- **Grounding Meditations:** Paying attention to the sensations of the feet on the floor, the hands resting in the lap, or other anchors in the present environment.
- **Body Scan with Permission:** Approaching body awareness with a sense of choice and the ability to shift focus if sensations become overwhelming.
- **Loving-Kindness for Self:** Directing gentle wishes of kindness and well-being towards oneself.

Important Considerations and Precautions:

While meditation offers significant benefits for addressing specific challenges, it's crucial to approach these practices with awareness and caution:

- **Not a Replacement for Professional Help:** Meditation should not be seen as a substitute for medical or psychological treatment. If you are experiencing significant mental or physical health challenges, it's essential to seek professional help.
- **Individual Differences:** Everyone's experience with meditation is unique. What works well for one person may not work for another. Be patient and experiment to find practices that resonate with you.
- **Potential for Emotional Arousal:** Some meditation practices, particularly when working with trauma or difficult emotions, can bring up intense feelings. It's important to proceed gently and with self-compassion, and to have support if needed.
- **Contraindications:** In rare cases, certain meditation practices might not be suitable for individuals with specific mental health conditions. Consult a healthcare professional or an experienced meditation teacher if you have concerns.
- **The Importance of Skilled Guidance:** When using meditation to address specific challenges, particularly trauma or severe mental health issues, working with a qualified and experienced meditation teacher or therapist who understands these conditions is highly recommended.

Meditation Journey

Meditation offers a powerful and adaptable toolkit for navigating the specific challenges that life can present. By intentionally applying mindfulness and other contemplative techniques, we can cultivate greater awareness, resilience, and inner resources to foster healing and transformation in areas where we struggle. However, it's essential to approach these practices with wisdom, self-compassion, and the understanding that they often work best in conjunction with other forms of support and treatment when dealing with significant health concerns. The journey of using meditation for transformation is personal, requiring patience, persistence, and a commitment to cultivating inner peace and well-being amidst life's inevitable difficulties.

Chapter 11: Deepening Your Meditation Practice: Cultivating Sustained Presence and Insight

Having established a consistent meditation practice, you may naturally seek ways to deepen your experience, cultivate more sustained presence, and unlock deeper levels of insight. Deepening your practice is not about achieving some extraordinary state or forcing profound experiences, but rather about refining your attention, cultivating greater sensitivity to your inner landscape, and allowing the natural unfolding of awareness to lead to richer understanding. This chapter will explore strategies and approaches for deepening your meditation practice, refining your technique, exploring different methods, cultivating supportive qualities, and navigating the nuances of sustained contemplative inquiry.

Refining Your Core Technique:

The foundation of a deeper practice often lies in the consistent and refined application of your chosen core technique, whether mindfulness of breath, body scan, loving-kindness, or another method.

- **Sharpening Your Attention:** Pay closer attention to the subtle nuances of your chosen object of focus. For breath awareness, this might involve noticing the precise point where you feel the breath most clearly, the subtle pauses between breaths, or the gentle expansion and contraction of your body. Body scans could involve noticing increasingly subtle sensations like tingling, warmth, or the absence of sensation.

- **Sustaining Focus with Less Effort:** As your practice matures, aim for a quality of sustained attention that is relaxed and effortless rather than strained or forced. Allow your attention to rest gently on the object without constant mental exertion.
- **Working with Distractions with Skill:** Instead of viewing distractions as failures, see them as opportunities to practice returning your attention gently. Notice the nature of your distractions – are they primarily thoughts, emotions, or sensory inputs? Observe how they arise and pass without getting caught in their content.
- **Cultivating Continuity:** Strive for continuity within your meditation session, minimizing the gaps where your mind wanders significantly. This doesn't mean eliminating all distractions, but rather developing the ability to return more swiftly and consistently to your focus.
- **Exploring Variations Within Your Technique:** Once you have a solid foundation, you can gently explore subtle variations within your chosen technique. For example, with breath awareness, you might shift your focus from the nostrils to the abdomen or observe the breath as a whole-body experience.

Exploring Different Meditation Methods:

Introducing new meditation techniques can offer fresh perspectives and deepen your understanding of contemplative practice.

- **Vipassanā (Insight Meditation):** If your primary practice has been Samatha (concentration-based), exploring Vipassanā techniques (as discussed in Chapter 2) can cultivate deeper insight into the nature of reality through mindful observation of impermanence, unsatisfactoriness, and non-self.
- **Loving-Kindness and Compassion (Heart Practices):** If your focus has been primarily on awareness, incorporating practices that cultivate positive emotions can open your heart and foster a greater sense of connection (as explored in Chapter 7).
- **Walking Meditation:** Integrating mindful movement can be particularly helpful for those who find sustained sitting challenging or for those who want to bring mindfulness into a different aspect of their experience (as discussed in Chapter 8).
- **Guided Meditations and Visualisations:** These can offer new ways to explore your inner landscape and target specific areas of growth or healing (as discussed in Chapter 9).
- **Transcendental Meditation (TM):** A mantra-based technique that promotes deep relaxation and altered states of consciousness.

- **Yoga Nidra:** A guided relaxation technique that induces a state of deep rest and can facilitate emotional and physical healing.
- **Zen Meditation (Zazen):** Emphasises "just sitting" with open awareness, cultivating presence without a specific object of focus.

When exploring new methods, approach them with curiosity and patience, allowing time to understand their unique principles and benefits.

Cultivating Supportive Qualities:

Certain inner qualities can significantly enhance and deepen your meditation practice:

- **Patience:** Progress in meditation is often gradual and non-linear. Cultivating patience with yourself and the process is essential. Avoid striving for specific outcomes or getting discouraged by perceived lack of progress.
- **Persistence:** Consistency is key to deepening your practice. Even short, regular sessions are more beneficial than infrequent, long ones. Maintain a commitment to your practice even when motivation wanes.
- **Curiosity:** Approach your meditation with a sense of open inquiry. Be curious about the subtle shifts in your body, mind, and emotions without judgment.
- **Acceptance:** Practice accepting whatever arises during your meditation – thoughts, feelings, distractions, states of restlessness or calm.

Resistance can create tension and hinder deeper awareness.

- **Kindness and Self-Compassion:** Treat yourself with kindness and understanding throughout your practice. Avoid self-criticism for mind-wandering or perceived failures. A gentle and compassionate attitude fosters a more receptive inner environment.
- **Discernment (Wisdom):** As your practice deepens, cultivate the ability to discern between passing thoughts and deeper insights, between reactivity and mindful response.

Navigating Deeper States and Experiences:

As your practice matures, you may encounter deeper states of concentration, altered perceptions, or insightful experiences. It's helpful to approach these with mindful awareness and a balanced perspective:

- **Deep Concentration (Jhana-like States):** You may experience profound stillness, absorption, and bliss. Observe these states without clinging to them or trying to recreate them. They are natural occurrences that can arise in a deepened practice.
- **Altered Perceptions:** You might notice changes in your perception of time, space, or body. Observe these phenomena with curiosity and without judgment, recognising them as potential shifts in your consciousness.
- **Insights and Understandings:** Deeper meditation can lead to profound insight into the nature of your mind, your patterns, and the

interconnectedness of things. Reflect on these insights after your meditation.

- **The "Dark Night of the Soul":** Some practitioners may experience challenging periods characterised by increased emotional intensity, feelings of unease, or a sense of disillusionment. Approach these periods with patience and self-compassion and potentially with the guidance of an experienced teacher. They can be part of the process of deeper transformation.
- **Non-Attachment to Experiences:** Regardless of the nature of your experiences in meditation, practice non-attachment. Clinging to pleasant states or resisting unpleasant ones can hinder further progress. Simply observe all experiences as temporary phenomena.

Deepening Your Practice Off the Cushion:

Extending the principles of meditation into your daily life is a crucial aspect of deepening your overall practice (as discussed in Chapter 6).

- **Mindfulness in Action:** Bring mindful awareness to everyday activities, paying attention to the sensations, thoughts, and emotions that arise.
- **Mindful Communication:** Practice listening and speaking with greater presence and awareness in your interactions with others.
- **Emotional Awareness Throughout the Day:** Notice your emotional states as they arise and pass, observing them with the same non-judgmental awareness you cultivate in formal practice.

- **Integrating Ethical Principles:** Living in alignment with ethical principles like non-harming, honesty, and generosity can create a more harmonious inner and outer environment that supports deeper contemplative practice.

Seeking Guidance and Community:

Connecting with experienced teachers and a supportive community can significantly aid in deepening your meditation practice.

- **Working with a Teacher:** A qualified meditation teacher can provide personalised guidance, address specific challenges, and offer insights based on their own experience and the wisdom of the tradition they represent.
- **Joining a Meditation Group or Community:** Practising with others can provide support, motivation, and a sense of shared journey. Group discussions and shared experiences can offer valuable perspectives.
- **Attending Retreats:** Longer periods of intensive practice in a retreat setting can provide an opportunity to deepen your concentration and insight in a focused and supportive environment.

The Ongoing Journey:

Deepening your meditation practice is not a destination but an ongoing journey of exploration, refinement, and self-discovery. Be patient, persistent, and kind to yourself along the way. Embrace the unfolding process with curiosity and a willingness to learn. The rewards of a deeper practice – greater presence, clarity, wisdom, and inner peace – are worth continued effort and dedication. Remember that the most profound insights often arise from consistent, gentle attention to the present moment, allowing the natural wisdom of your own awareness to unfold.

Chapter 12: The Scientific Landscape of Meditation: Unveiling the Evidence

Meditation has been understood through personal experience, philosophical inquiry, and spiritual tradition for centuries. However, the last few decades have witnessed an explosion of scientific interest in exploring the mechanisms and effects of these ancient practices using the rigorous tools of modern neuroscience, psychology, and medicine. This chapter will delve into the burgeoning scientific landscape of meditation research, examining the methodologies employed, the key findings across various domains of human functioning, and the ongoing efforts to understand the profound impact of contemplative practices on the brain, body, and mind.

The Rise of Scientific Inquiry into Meditation:

The increasing interest in the scientific study of meditation can be attributed to several converging factors:

- **Growing Popularity and Accessibility:** As meditation became more mainstream in Western cultures, researchers were naturally curious about its purported benefits and underlying mechanisms.
- **Advancements in Neuroimaging Technologies:** The development of sophisticated brain imaging techniques such as electroencephalography (EEG), functional magnetic

resonance imaging (FMRI), and magnetoencephalography (MEG) allowed scientists to observe brain activity in meditators in real-time, providing unprecedented insights into the neural correlates of contemplative states.

- **Interdisciplinary Collaboration:** The field has fostered increasing collaboration between neuroscientists, psychologists, physicians, and experienced meditation practitioners, leading to more nuanced and comprehensive research.
- **Recognition of the Limitations of Conventional Approaches:** In areas like stress management, mental health, and chronic pain, the limitations of traditional medical interventions spurred the exploration of complementary and alternative therapies like meditation.
- **Funding Initiatives:** Growing recognition of meditation's potential public health benefits has led to increased funding for scientific research from government agencies and private foundations.

Methodologies Employed in Meditation Research:

The scientific investigation of meditation utilizes a diverse array of research methodologies:

- **Neuroimaging Studies (fMRI, EEG, MEG):** These techniques allow researchers to measure brain activity (blood flow, electrical oscillations) during meditation, identifying changes in specific brain regions and networks associated with different meditative states and long-term practice.

- **Psychophysiological Measures:** Researchers often employ measures like heart rate variability (HRV), skin conductance response (SCR), and cortisol levels to assess the impact of meditation on the autonomic nervous system and stress response.
- **Randomised Controlled Trials (RCTS): Considered the gold standard in medical research, RCTS** involve randomly assigning participants to either a meditation intervention group or a control group (e.g., waitlist, active control) to assess the efficacy of meditation for specific outcomes.
- **Longitudinal Studies:** These studies track the effects of meditation practice over extended periods, providing insights into the long-term impact on brain structure, function, and psychological well-being.
- **Meta-Analyses:** These studies combine the results of multiple independent studies to provide a more robust and comprehensive overview of the evidence for the effectiveness of meditation for specific outcomes.
- **Qualitative Research:** Interviews and focus groups with meditators can provide valuable insights into their subjective experiences and the perceived benefits of practice.

Key Findings Across Various Domains:

The growing body of scientific research has revealed significant and promising findings regarding the impact of meditation across various aspects of human functioning:

Brain Structure and Function:

- **Increased Grey Matter Density:** Studies have shown that long-term meditation practice is associated with increased grey matter volume in brain regions involved in attention, self-awareness, compassion, and emotional regulation, such as the prefrontal cortex, hippocampus, and insula.
- **Reduced Amygdala Volume and Activity:** The amygdala, the brain's primary centre for processing fear and threat, is smaller and less reactive in experienced meditators, suggesting a reduced stress response.
- **Enhanced Brain Connectivity:** Research indicates increased functional and structural connectivity between different brain regions, particularly between the prefrontal cortex and areas involved in emotion regulation, suggesting improved self-control and emotional stability.
- **Changes in Brainwave Activity (EEG):** EEG studies have consistently shown increased alpha and theta brainwave activity during meditation, which are associated with relaxation, focused attention, and altered states of consciousness. Gamma wave activity, linked to higher-order cognitive processing and integration, has also increased in experienced meditators.

Stress Reduction and Mental Health:

- **Reduced Cortisol Levels:** Studies have demonstrated that meditation, particularly MBSR and related interventions, can significantly reduce the stress hormone cortisol.
- **Improved Symptoms of Anxiety and Depression:** Numerous RCTS and meta-analyses have shown the efficacy of mindfulness-based interventions in reducing symptoms of anxiety disorders (generalised anxiety, social anxiety, panic disorder) and mild to moderate depression.
- **Prevention of Depressive Relapse:** MBCT has been shown to be effective in preventing relapse in individuals with recurrent depression.
- **Improved Emotional Regulation:** Meditation practice is associated with an increased ability to observe and manage emotions without overreacting.
- **Reduced Symptoms of PTSD:** Some research suggests that trauma-informed mindfulness practices can be beneficial in reducing symptoms of post-traumatic stress disorder.

Attention and Cognitive Function:

Meditation Journey

- **Enhanced Sustained Attention:** Studies have shown that regular meditation can improve the ability to focus and maintain attention over time.
- **Improved Working Memory:** Some research suggests that meditation can enhance working memory capacity.
- **Increased Cognitive Flexibility:** Meditation may improve the ability to shift between different tasks or mental sets.
- **Reduced Mind-Wandering:** Mindfulness practices directly target the tendency for the mind to wander, leading to greater presence and focus.

Pain Management:

- **Reduced Perceived Pain Intensity:** Mindfulness meditation has been shown to help individuals cope with chronic pain by shifting their attention and reducing emotional reactivity to pain sensations.
- **Improved Functional Capacity:** By reducing the psychological distress associated with chronic pain, meditation can lead to improvements in daily functioning.

Sleep:

- **Improved Sleep Quality:** Mindfulness-based interventions have been found to improve sleep quality, reduce sleep onset latency (the time it takes to fall asleep), and increase total sleep time in individuals with insomnia.

Compassion and Prosocial Behaviour:

- **Increased Empathy and Compassion:** Studies using loving-kindness and compassion meditation have shown increases in self-reported empathy and compassion and changes in brain regions associated with these emotions.
- **Increased Prosocial Behaviour:** Some research suggests a link between compassion meditation and increased willingness to help others.

Ageing and Longevity:

- **Preservation of Grey Matter:** Preliminary research suggests that long-term meditators may experience less age-related decline in grey matter volume in certain brain regions.
- **Telomere Length:** Some studies have explored the potential link between meditation and longer telomere length, a biomarker associated with cellular ageing and longevity. However, more research is needed in this area.

Mechanisms of Action: How Does Meditation Work?

While the precise mechanisms by which meditation exerts its effects are still being investigated, several key pathways have been identified:

- **Attention Regulation:** Meditation trains the ability to focus and sustain attention, disengage from distractions, and redirect focus. This strengthening of attentional control likely underlies many of the cognitive benefits.
- **Emotional Regulation:** Meditation helps to break the cycle of automatic emotional responses by cultivating non-reactive awareness of emotions. Increased prefrontal cortex activity and reduced amygdala reactivity contribute to greater emotional stability.
- **Body Awareness (interoception):** Practices like body scans enhance awareness of internal bodily sensations, which can improve self-regulation and the ability to recognise and respond to bodily cues related to stress, pain, and emotions.
- **Changes in Self-Perception:** Meditation can lead to a more decentred perspective on thoughts and emotions, recognising them as transient mental events rather than fixed aspects of the self. This can reduce identification with negative self-talk and promote greater psychological flexibility.
- **Relaxation Response:** Many meditation techniques elicit the relaxation response, which is characterised by decreased heart rate, blood

pressure, and muscle tension. This response counteracts the physiological effects of stress.
- **Neuroplasticity:** The brain's ability to change its structure and function in response to experience, known as neuroplasticity, is believed to be a key mechanism by which long-term meditation practice leads to lasting changes in brain structure and connectivity.

Challenges and Future Directions in Meditation Research:

Despite the significant progress made, the scientific study of meditation still faces several challenges:

- **Defining and Standardising Meditation Practices:** The vast array of meditation techniques and variations makes it challenging to standardise interventions and compare results across studies.
- **Controlling for Placebo Effects:** It can be difficult to create truly inert control groups in meditation research, as the expectation of benefit and the attention received by participants in intervention groups can influence outcomes. Active control groups (e.g., relaxation training) are increasingly being used.
- **Understanding Dosage and Specificity:** More research is needed to determine the optimal "dose" of meditation (frequency, duration, intensity) for different outcomes and identify the most effective techniques for particular challenges.
- **Investigating Long-Term Effects:** While some longitudinal studies exist, more research is

needed to fully understand the long-term impact of sustained meditation practice on brain health, ageing, and well-being.

- **Exploring Individual Differences:** People respond to meditation in different ways. Future research should investigate individual factors that may predict who is most likely to benefit from specific types of meditation.
- **Bridging Subjective Experience and Objective Measures:** Integrating first-person accounts of meditative experiences with objective neuroscientific and physiological data remains a key challenge and opportunity.
- **Ethical Considerations:** As meditation becomes more integrated into healthcare and other settings, ethical considerations regarding accessibility, potential for misuse, and the framing of meditation need careful attention.

Future research in meditation science promises to illuminate further the intricate relationship between contemplative practices and human well-being. By refining methodologies, exploring diverse traditions, and investigating the underlying mechanisms with increasing precision, scientists can contribute to a more comprehensive understanding of meditation's transformative potential and inform its optimal application in various contexts. This growing body of evidence validates ancient traditions' wisdom and paves the way for integrating mindfulness and other contemplative practices into mainstream healthcare, education, and society, offering powerful tools for cultivating a healthier and more mindful world.

Meditation Journey

Book titles from PAB Publications available on Amazon

Transform Your Parenting Journey and Raise Mindful, Resilient, and Compassionate Children in the Digital Age.

"No Buy Made Easy: A Practical Guide to Sustainable Living and Conscious Choices" is your essential roadmap to breaking free from consumerism and embracing a more fulfilling, affordable, and eco-friendly lifestyle.

"Climate Change Made Easy" cuts through the jargon and delivers a clear, accessible guide to the most pressing issue of our time. This book empowers you with the knowledge to understand the science behind global warming, its real-world impacts, and the hopeful solutions within our reach.

Dive into the exhilarating and heart-pounding adventure of "Dolphins of Expedor"! Meet Timothy Shore, a remarkable fourteen-year-old yellow dolphin with the gift of speech, as he is thrust into a perilous whirlpool of destiny to save his cherished underwater city, Expedor, from the brink of annihilation.

Meditation Journey

STELLA WISE COLLECTION
SPIRITUAL INSPIRATION & CREATIVITY

EXPLORE THE COLLECTION

Lawrence Finch

STELLA WISE COLLECTION
SPIRITUAL INSPIRATION & CREATIVITY

EXPLORE THE COLLECTION

Printed in Great Britain
by Amazon